HOW THINGS WORK

HOW FLOATING MACHINES WORK

IAN GRAHAM

Kingfisher Books

Kingfisher Books, Grisewood & Dempsey Ltd, Elsley House,
24-30 Great Titchfield Street, London W1P 7AD

First published in 1993 by Kingfisher Books
2 4 6 8 10 9 7 5 3
Copyright © Grisewood & Dempsey Ltd 1993

BRITISH LIBRARY CATALOGUING IN PUBLICATION DATA
A catalogue record for this book is available from
the British Library

ISBN 0 86272 771 5

Typeset in 3B2
Phototypeset by Southern Positives and Negatives (SPAN),
Lingfield, Surrey
Printed and bound in Hong Kong

Series editor: Jackie Gaff
Series designer: David West Children's Books
Author: Ian Graham
Cover illustration: Micheal Fisher (Garden Studio)
Illustrators: Peter Bull pp. 14-15; Chris Forsey pp. 6-9,
18-19, 22-3; Mike Saunders pp. 30-1; Simon Tegg pp. 24-7,
32-3, 36-7; Ian Thompson pp. 2-5, 10-11; Ross Watton
(Garden Studio) pp. 12-13, 16-17, 20-1, 28-9, 34-5, 38-9.
Research: A.R. Blann

The publishers would like to thank: David Jefferis;
Camper and Nicholsons (Yachts) Ltd; Chas Newens Marine
Co. Ltd; Dover Port Authority; Fletcher International
Sportsboats; GEC Plessey; Hoverspeed; Kawasaki Jet Ski
Europe; MOD (Royal Navy); P&O European Ferries;
Quicksilver Marine Parts; Racal Marine Electronics; Vickers
Shipbuilding & Engineering Ltd; Virgin Group Ltd; Vosper
Thornycroft (UK) Ltd; Watercraft World Ltd; Woods Hole
Oceanographic Institution.

CONTENTS

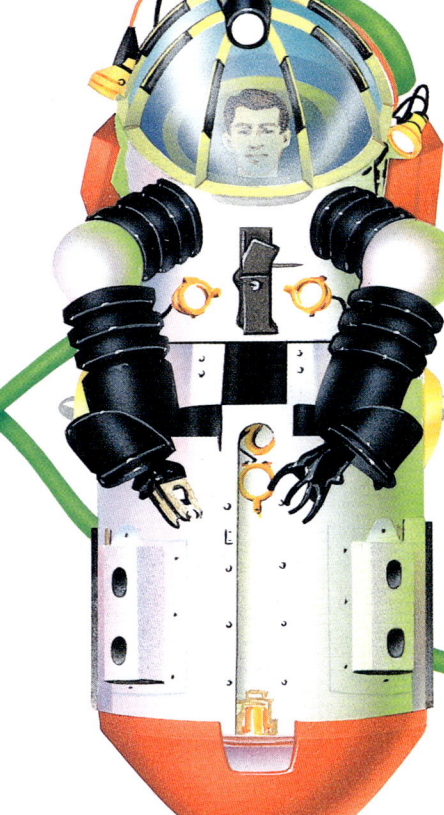

FAMOUS FLOATING FIRSTS

▽ Our earliest records of ships date back to about 3500 BC, and come from Egyptian paintings and documents. Ships had square sails and were steered by oars.

▽ In the 1st century AD, the rudder was invented in China. It had reached the West by the 1200s.

▽ By about AD 100, Arab sailors had invented a triangular sail (later known as a lateen sail), which allowed ships to sail into the wind.

▽ In the 1490s, Christopher Columbus' sailors learnt how to sleep in hammocks, after seeing hanging beds called *hamacas* in the West Indies.

△ In the 1770s, the English explorer Captain James Cook wrote about people surfing in Hawaii.

△ In 1776, the first attack was made by a military submarine, the USS *Turtle*.

△ In 1802, the world's first reliable steamship, the *Charlotte Dundas*, went into service in Scotland.

△ In 1836-37, screw propellers were patented by John Ericsson in the USA and Francis Pettit Smith in the UK.

▽ In 1897, Englishman Charles A. Parsons' *Turbinia* became the first ship to be powered by a steam turbine.

▽ In 1900, in the USA, Irishman John P. Holland built the first modern submarine.

▽ In 1906, Enrico Forlanini of Italy tested the first successful hydrofoil.

▽ In 1922, water-skis were invented by Ralph Samuelson.

△ In the 1940s, sailboarding was invented in Florida, USA.

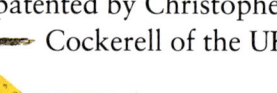

△ In 1955, the first nuclear-powered vessel, the US submarine *Nautilus*, put to sea.

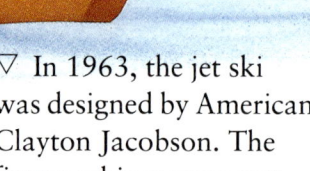

△ In 1959, the first hovercraft flight was made, by the SR.N1 from the Isle of Wight. The machine was patented by Christopher Cockerell of the UK.

▽ In 1963, the jet ski was designed by American Clayton Jacobson. The first machines were put on sale in 1973.

INTRODUCTION

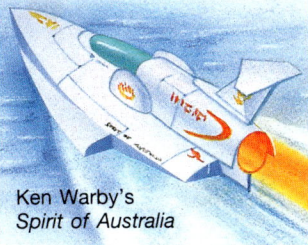

Led by the need to find food, or just curiosity, people have always explored the world around them. Our ancestors probably made their first journeys on water by floating out into rivers and bays on top of tree trunks. As long as 10,000 years ago, they had learnt to make simple boats called dug-outs by hollowing out tree trunks.

Many thousands of years later people discovered that boats could be built by joining wooden planks together. Boats could now be any shape or size. Small ones were pushed along by paddles or oars, but larger ones needed the power of wind pushing against sails to propel them.

All the great voyages of exploration were made by sailing ships. Then, in the 1800s, the invention of the steam engine opened up a new source of power and led to new designs. In this century, new materials and small powerful engines have made lightweight yachts and motorboats possible. And the popularity of water sports has led to the invention of water-skis, the sailboard and the jet ski.

Donald Campbell's *Bluebird*

Motorboat racing was made possible by the invention of the petrol engine in the 1880s. In 1904, motorboats were reaching over 30 km/h. The jet engine was invented in 1930, and in 1939 Britain's Malcolm Campbell sped to 227 km/h in a jet-powered hydroplane. In 1964, Campbell's son Donald reached 444 km/h.

Ken Warby's *Spirit of Australia*

Today, the official world water speed record is 514 km/h. It was set by Australian Ken Warby in a jet-powered hydroplane, in 1978. His unofficial top speed is 556 km/h.

The fastest sailing craft in the world today are sailboards. They have reached speeds greater than 80 km/h.

Water has pressure or push, which increases with depth (turn to page 34 for the reasons pressure becomes greater the deeper you go).

   If something is thrown into water, the water presses against it from all directions – from above, from the sides, and from below. But because the pressure is greater in deeper water, the water below the object pushes up harder than the water above it pushes down. This difference in pressure creates upthrust. If the upthrust can overcome its weight, the object will float.

FLOATING & SINKING

Have you ever wondered why wooden twigs float on water but pebbles sink? Well, when something falls into water, it presses down on it. The water pushes back with a force called upthrust. If the upthrust is greater than the object's weight, the object is pushed upwards. At the water's surface, upthrust and weight balance, and the object floats.

   The ability to float is called buoyancy. A wooden twig floats because the water's upthrust overcomes the twig's weight. A pebble sinks because its weight is greater than the upthrust.

☐ DEAD WOOD

When a tree is cut down and dies, all the microscopically tiny tubes that carried water and food from the soil to the leaves fill with air. The air helps to make the logs light enough to float.

☐ LOGGING

In some parts of the world, tree trunks are floated down river from the forests where they grow, to the sawmills where they are cut up. Workers balance on the logs to push them on their way.

MATERIALS

The earliest boats were made from wood and reeds, but few modern boats are still made from these natural materials. Plastics and metals are now more common.

TEST IT OUT!

To see the effect of upthrust, drop small objects into water. Heavy things will sink because their weight is greater than the water's upthrust. Light things will float because the upthrust overcomes their weight.

LIGHTWEIGHT BOATS

Our ancestors probably began making boats after noticing that wood floats. They hollowed out tree trunks to make canoes or lashed them together into rafts. In marshy areas, where the tall grasses called reeds grew, people learned to shape bundles of reeds into boats.

Canoes made by hollowing out tree trunks are called dug-outs

Reed boats are still made and used in some parts of the world today

Planks are lighter than whole tree trunks and so make better rafts

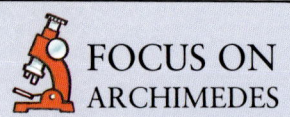

Archimedes was a Greek mathematician who lived from about 287 to 212 BC. He made an important discovery about buoyancy, when in his bath.

As he got in, some water spilled out. Archimedes noticed that his body seemed to weigh less in water than it did in air. He decided that this loss of weight must be equal to the weight of the water spilled, or displaced. Another way of putting Archimedes' Principle is to say that the push of the water's upthrust is equal to the weight of water displaced.

HULLS & DISPLACEMENT

Buoyancy is affected by shape as well as weight. A boat with a hull – a wide bottom and tall sides – can carry more weight than a raft. This is partly because it can settle lower in the water without sinking. And the lower the boat settles, the greater the upthrust pushing on it from below.

As it settles lower, the boat is also pushing aside water. This 'pushing aside' is called displacement. The boat will float as long as the water's upthrust is equal to the weight of the water the boat displaces.

☐ KEEPING THE BALANCE

The paddler's weight helps to press the kayak down into the water. The lower the kayak settles, the greater the water's upthrust. It will float as long as the upthrust equals the water displaced.

Stern

☐ BUILT FOR STRENGTH

The hull of a long ship such as an oil tanker is divided into compartments. Their walls brace the hull and stop it twisting along its length. They also stop the oil from sloshing around too much.

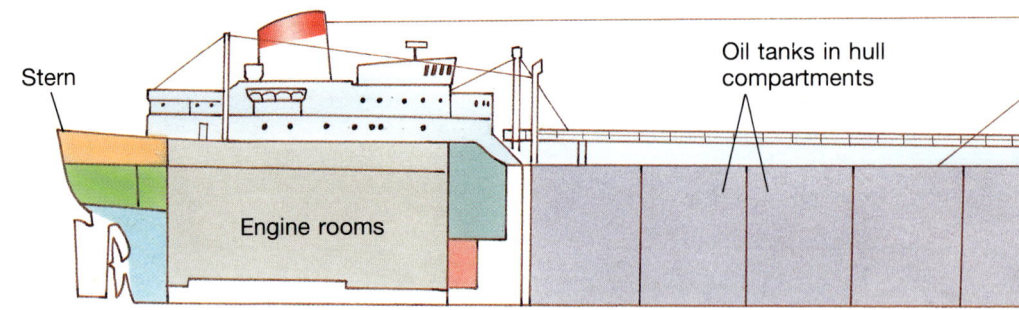

Stern

Oil tanks in hull compartments

Engine rooms

PADDLING

Kayaks are propelled through the water by paddles and muscle power. Pulling the paddle back through the water makes the kayak move forwards. When the paddle is pushed forwards, the kayak goes backwards.

Paddle blade is broad so it catches as much water as possible

TEST IT OUT!

Here's a way to test the effect of hull shape on buoyancy. Roll a fist-sized piece of modelling clay into a ball and drop it into a bowl of water. It will sink like a stone – straight to the bottom of the bowl!

Next take the clay out and mould it into a new shape. Press the ball flat, then pull up the edges and join them into a hull.

Your boat will float now. The clay weighs the same as before, but its new shape lets it displace more water.

STAYING AFLOAT

Kayaks often have blocks of a special foam inside the bow (front) and stern (back). The foam traps tiny bubbles of air inside it, and this helps to stop the kayak from filling with water and sinking if it is holed.

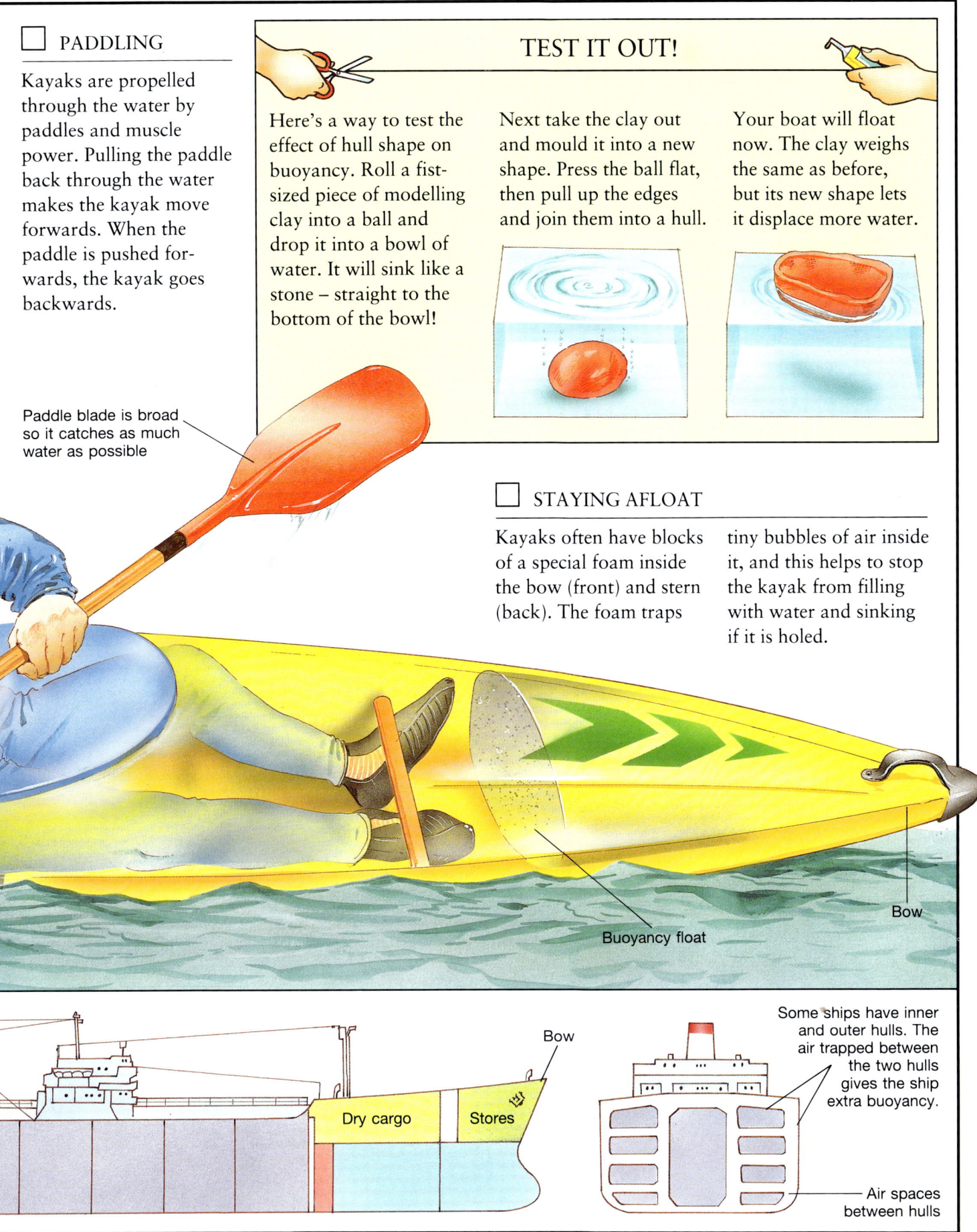

Buoyancy float

Bow

Bow

Dry cargo

Stores

Some ships have inner and outer hulls. The air trapped between the two hulls gives the ship extra buoyancy.

Air spaces between hulls

CATCHING THE WIND

Sails allow boats to be driven by the wind. Usually, the bigger and heavier the boat, the greater the number of sails. The biggest of the old ships still in service today have more than 30 sails. A crew of over 200 people is needed to raise, lower and manage them.

Changing a sail's shape and angle to the wind is called trimming. It is done by pulling on ropes, which are called sheets on boats. Trimming alters the forces acting on the sail and allows the crew to control the boat's speed.

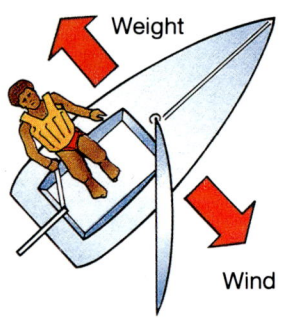

Weight

Wind

The word moment has more than one meaning. Besides being a short time, it is also a force that turns something. The moment of a force is equal to the size of the force multiplied by its distance from the thing that turns.

Wind pushing on a boat's sail creates a moment which tries to tip the boat over. The sailor can create a moment in the opposite direction by leaning out from the side of the boat.

☐ BALANCING ACT

As the wind fills the sail, it tries to push the sail and the boat over. The sailors lean out, to use their weight to stop the wind from heeling (tipping) the boat over too far. The further they lean, the more their weight balances the wind's push.

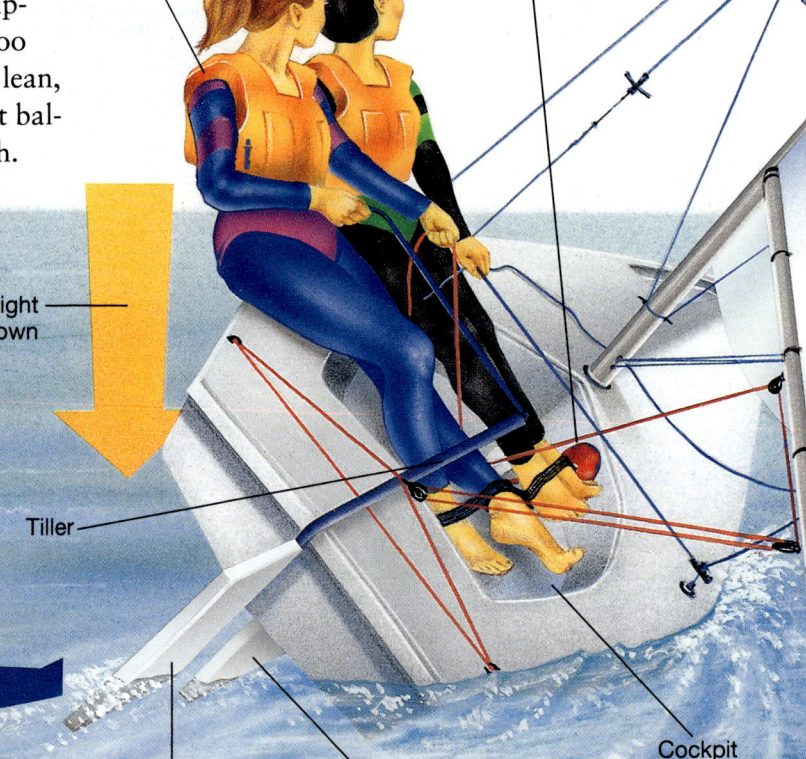

Mainsheet

Body weight pushes down

Tiller

Rudder

Daggerboard

Cockpit

☐ PUSHING BACK

When the boat heels, the rudder and daggerboard are pulled up through the water. The water resists (fights back), pushing down on the top of them. This resistance helps to reduce the effect of the wind, as it tries to push the sail over.

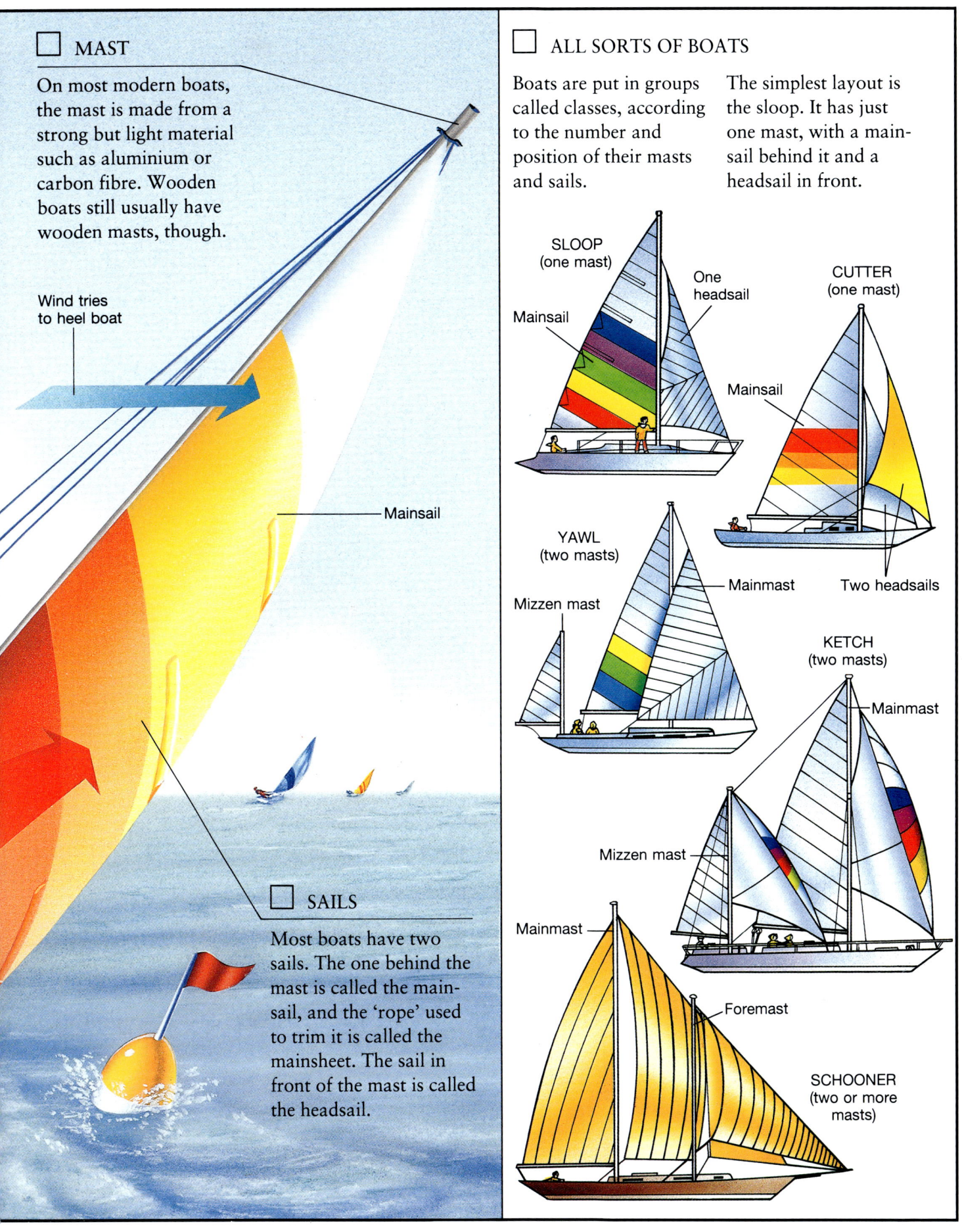

☐ MAST

On most modern boats, the mast is made from a strong but light material such as aluminium or carbon fibre. Wooden boats still usually have wooden masts, though.

Wind tries to heel boat

Mainsail

☐ SAILS

Most boats have two sails. The one behind the mast is called the mainsail, and the 'rope' used to trim it is called the mainsheet. The sail in front of the mast is called the headsail.

☐ ALL SORTS OF BOATS

Boats are put in groups called classes, according to the number and position of their masts and sails.

The simplest layout is the sloop. It has just one mast, with a mainsail behind it and a headsail in front.

SLOOP
(one mast)

One headsail

Mainsail

CUTTER
(one mast)

Mainsail

YAWL
(two masts)

Mizzen mast

Mainmast

Two headsails

KETCH
(two masts)

Mainmast

Mizzen mast

Mainmast

Foremast

SCHOONER
(two or more masts)

FOCUS ON SLOT EFFECT

Two sails can be set at an angle to the wind, and with just a narrow slot between them at the place where they overlap each other. As air squeezes through this slot, it speeds up. The faster air rushing across the mainsail magnifies the suction force the sail creates, making the boat go even faster.

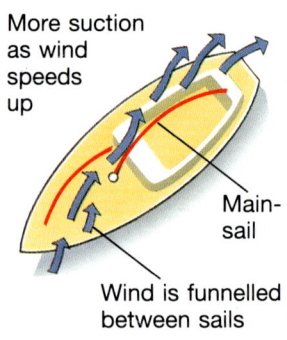

More suction as wind speeds up

Main-sail

Wind is funnelled between sails

There are two ways that sails can catch and use the power of the wind. Firstly, they can be set so that the wind blows directly into them, from behind. The wind pushes the sails, and they carry the boat with them. Propelled in this way, boats can only travel in the same direction as the wind.

But if sails are set so that the wind comes at them from an angle, a boat can head in almost any direction. The air now flows across both sides of the sails, instead of just filling them. The divided air thrusts the boat onwards, and creates a suction force which helps to increase speed.

1 AEROFOILS & SUCTION

Wind is moving air, and its pressure lowers with speed. The wind flowing round the outside of an aerofoil-shaped sail moves faster and has less pressure than that flowing across the inside. The difference in air pressure creates a force that tries to suck the sail (and boat) forwards and sideways.

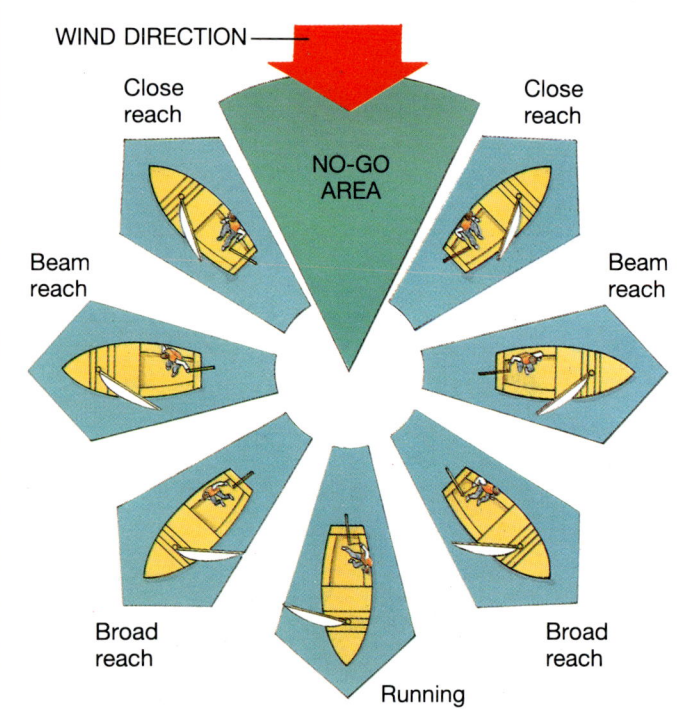

WIND DIRECTION

Close reach

NO-GO AREA

Close reach

Beam reach

Beam reach

Broad reach

Broad reach

Running

☐ SAILING

All the different angles to the wind in which a boat can move are called the points of sailing.

Sailing with the wind blowing from the side is known as reaching. Sailing with it behind, pushing the boat along, is called running.

A boat can never sail directly into the wind, so there is a no-go area. When a boat is sailing as close to the no-go area as possible it is said to be close-hauled.

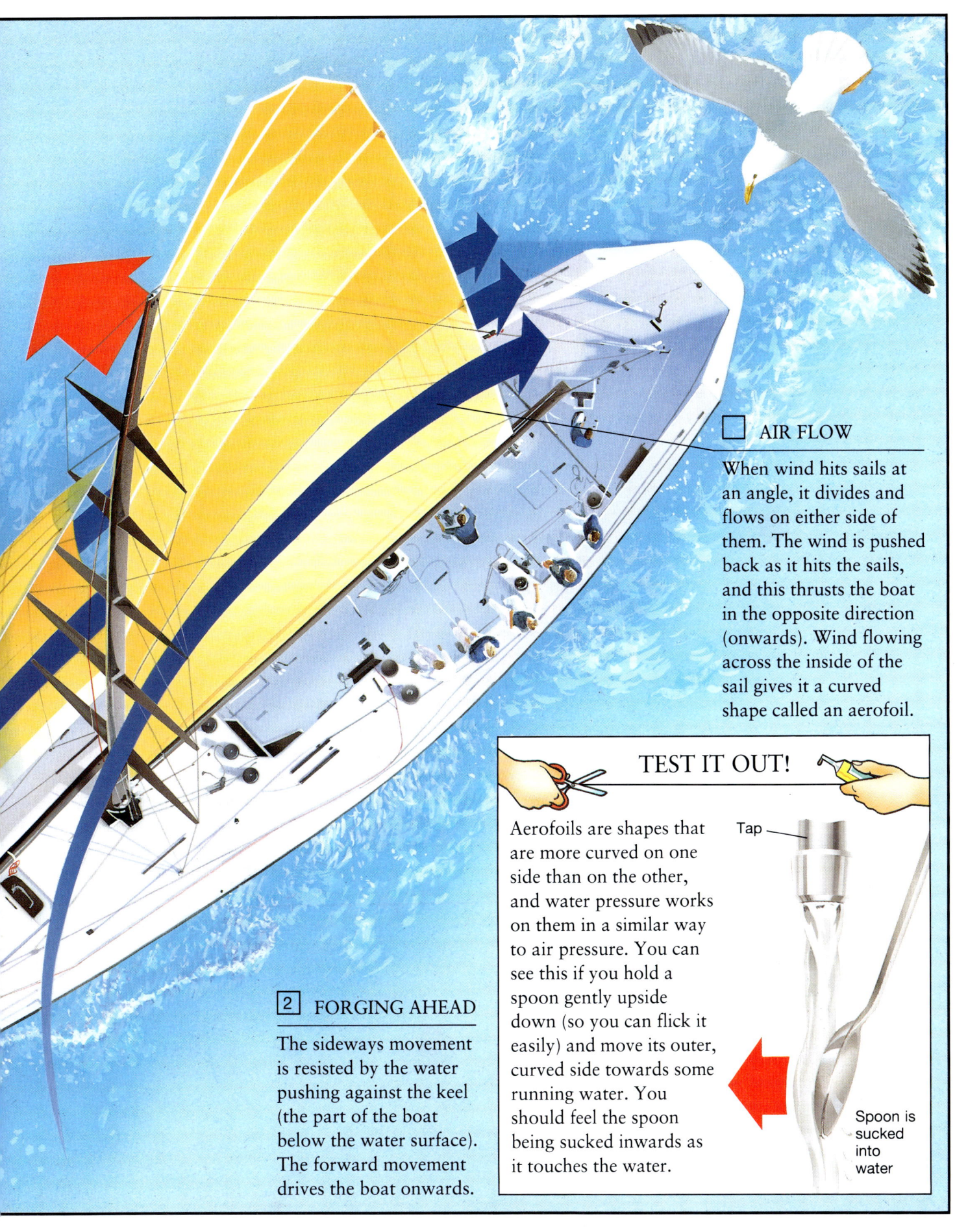

AIR FLOW

When wind hits sails at an angle, it divides and flows on either side of them. The wind is pushed back as it hits the sails, and this thrusts the boat in the opposite direction (onwards). Wind flowing across the inside of the sail gives it a curved shape called an aerofoil.

2 FORGING AHEAD

The sideways movement is resisted by the water pushing against the keel (the part of the boat below the water surface). The forward movement drives the boat onwards.

TEST IT OUT!

Aerofoils are shapes that are more curved on one side than on the other, and water pressure works on them in a similar way to air pressure. You can see this if you hold a spoon gently upside down (so you can flick it easily) and move its outer, curved side towards some running water. You should feel the spoon being sucked inwards as it touches the water.

Tap

Spoon is sucked into water

STEERING & RUDDERS

No matter how big or small they are, or whether they are propelled by wind or engine power, most boats are steered by the pressure (pushing force) of water acting against the rudder. When the rudder is turned, the pressure of the water becomes greater on one side of it than on the other. This pushes the stern sideways and brings the bow round.

Big boats have a steering wheel, but in small boats a handle called a tiller is used to move the rudder (you can see one on page 10).

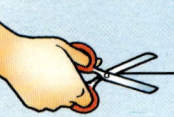

TEST IT OUT!

Ask a grown-up to help you cut a polystyrene tile into a boat shape, with three rudder slots. Make a paper sail, then push a stick through it and into the boat. Now cut a rudder out of the plastic-coated card from a juice carton.

Fix the rudder in one of the stern slots and put your boat in water. Which direction does the boat head in when you blow into the sail?

Move the rudder and blow again. The boat should head in a different direction!

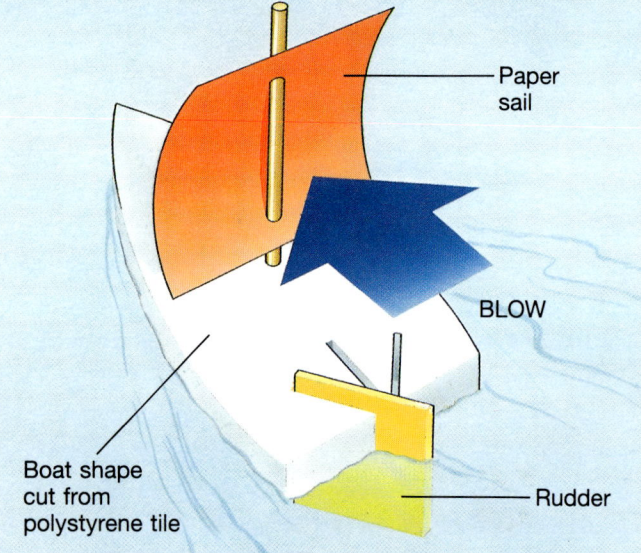

Paper sail

BLOW

Boat shape cut from polystyrene tile

Rudder

☐ STEERING GEAR

In a big boat, the wheel is linked to the rudder by pulleys and cables. A pulley is a wheel with a grooved rim which holds the cable in. Turning the wheel to the left tightens the lefthand cable, pulling the rudder in the same direction.

☐ RUDDER

The rudder pivots (turns) at the point where it is fitted to the stern of the boat. The further the steering wheel is turned, the further the rudder moves.

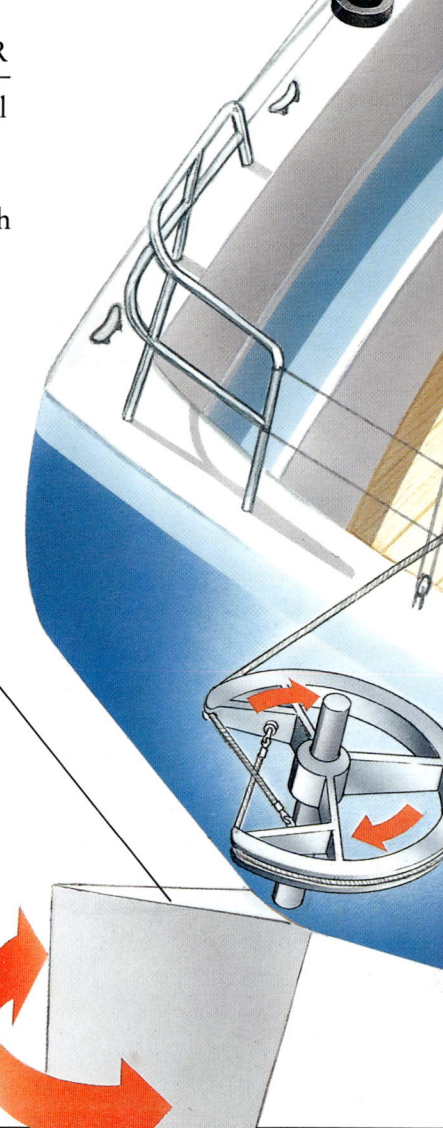

Rudder pivots from left to right

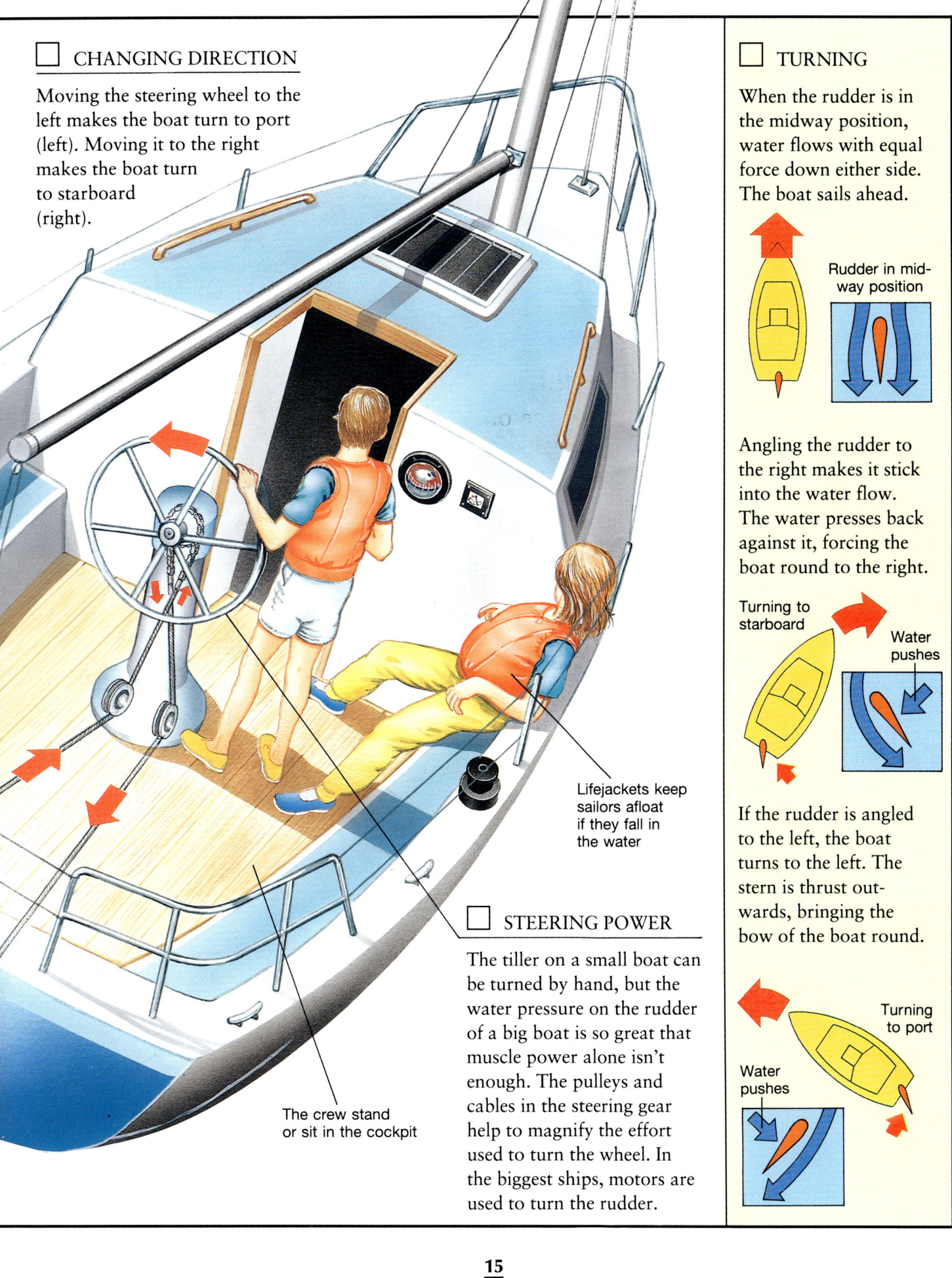

☐ CHANGING DIRECTION

Moving the steering wheel to the left makes the boat turn to port (left). Moving it to the right makes the boat turn to starboard (right).

☐ TURNING

When the rudder is in the midway position, water flows with equal force down either side. The boat sails ahead.

Rudder in mid-way position

Angling the rudder to the right makes it stick into the water flow. The water presses back against it, forcing the boat round to the right.

Turning to starboard

Water pushes

If the rudder is angled to the left, the boat turns to the left. The stern is thrust outwards, bringing the bow of the boat round.

Turning to port

Water pushes

Lifejackets keep sailors afloat if they fall in the water

The crew stand or sit in the cockpit

☐ STEERING POWER

The tiller on a small boat can be turned by hand, but the water pressure on the rudder of a big boat is so great that muscle power alone isn't enough. The pulleys and cables in the steering gear help to magnify the effort used to turn the wheel. In the biggest ships, motors are used to turn the rudder.

FOCUS ON PROPULSION

When the first ships with engines were built, paddle-wheels were used to propel them. As the wheels turned, their paddles pushed against the water. Water resistance drove the ship forwards. By 1840, propellers were replacing paddle-wheels.

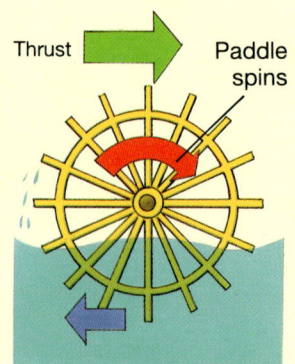

Thrust   Paddle spins

As a propeller spins, its blades push back against the water like paddles. At the same time, the aerofoil-shaped blades work like underwater sails. A difference in the pressure of the water on either side of the blades creates suction.

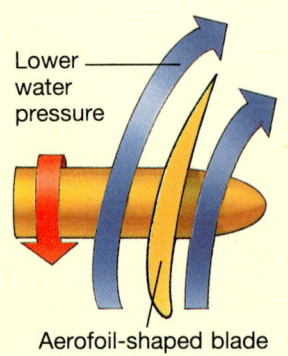

Lower water pressure

Aerofoil-shaped blade

Engine power has one advantage over sail power. It means boats can go anywhere at any time, because they don't have to rely on there being enough wind to blow them along! Most boats with engines are pushed through the water by one or more propellers. These are driven by the engine, and connected to it by a propeller shaft.

As a propeller spins, its blades screw their way through the water, pushing it backwards. This thrusts the boat in the opposite direction – forwards. At the same time, however, the boat is being sucked forwards. The suction force is created because the propeller blades are aerofoil shaped and work rather like underwater wings.

☐ AIR BOATS

Underwater propellers cannot be used in swamps and other places where the water is shallow or full of weeds. Air boats driven by aircraft propellers are used instead. Their flattened hulls don't sit low in the water.

Aircraft propeller

Rudder

Flat hull for skimming over water

☐ BOW & STERN THRUSTERS

Car ferries and other types of big ship often have propellers called thrusters. These move the ship by pushing water out to the side of it. Thrusters let ships dock in tight spaces.

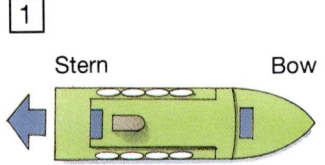

1 Stern   Bow

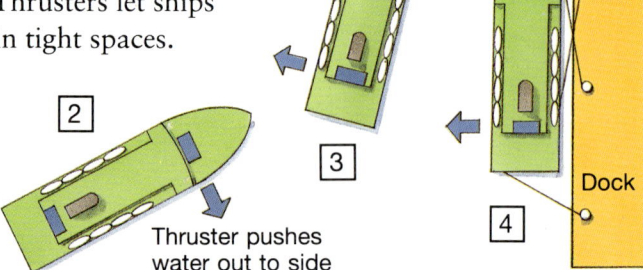

2

Thruster pushes water out to side

3

4

Dock

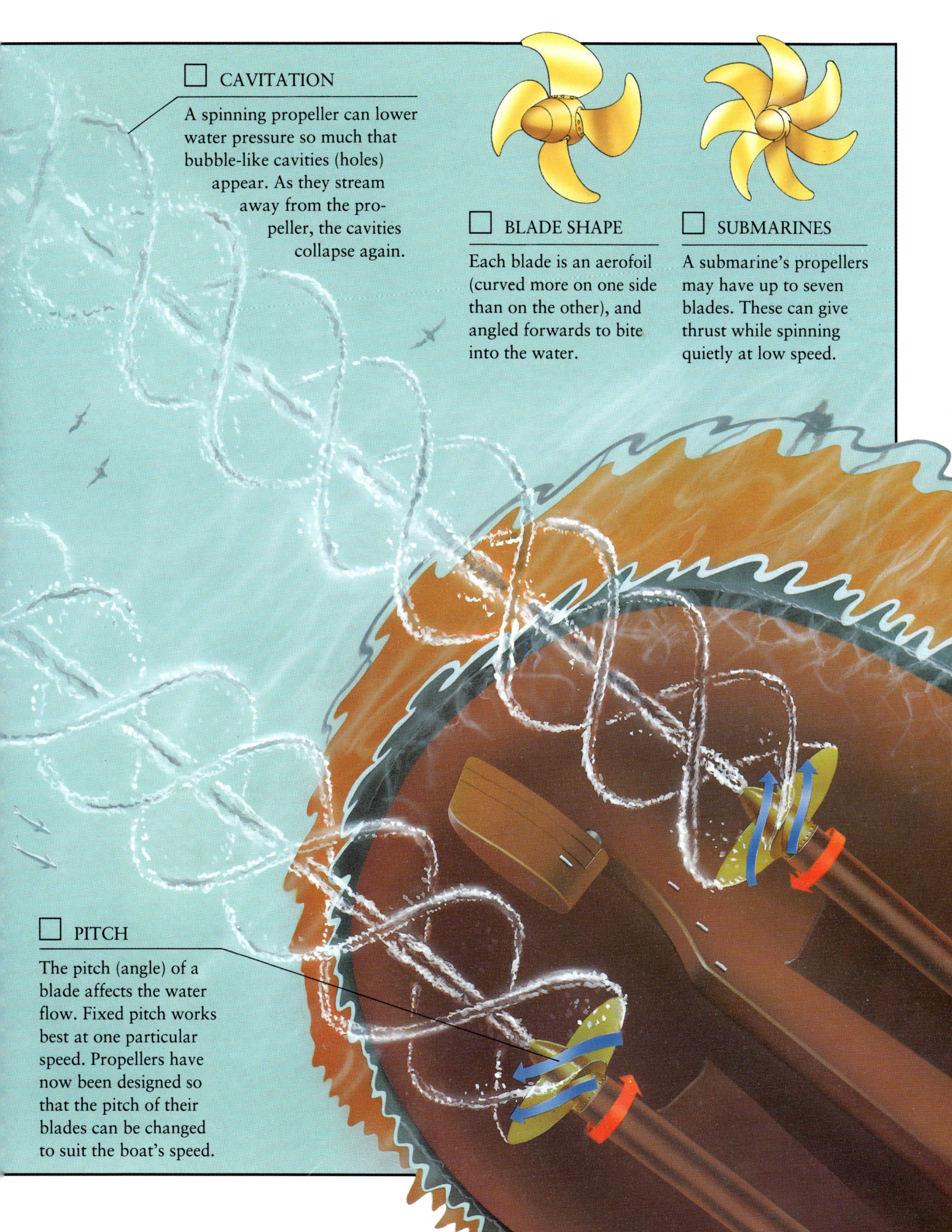

☐ CAVITATION

A spinning propeller can lower water pressure so much that bubble-like cavities (holes) appear. As they stream away from the propeller, the cavities collapse again.

☐ BLADE SHAPE

Each blade is an aerofoil (curved more on one side than on the other), and angled forwards to bite into the water.

☐ SUBMARINES

A submarine's propellers may have up to seven blades. These can give thrust while spinning quietly at low speed.

☐ PITCH

The pitch (angle) of a blade affects the water flow. Fixed pitch works best at one particular speed. Propellers have now been designed so that the pitch of their blades can be changed to suit the boat's speed.

JET SKIS – WATER POWER

Jet-skiing is like a cross between water-skiing and motor-cycling. It's become a popular sport since the first machines were sold in the early 1970s. A jet ski is propelled by the thrust from a powerful jet of water. This jet is produced by an engine-driven impeller.

A jet ski's impeller looks and works rather like a propeller inside a pipe. As it spins, it sucks in water, speeds it up, and then forces it out again. The faster the impeller spins, the more powerful the water jet it produces, and the faster the jet ski scoots along.

Water-jet engines work in much the same way as rocket or jet aircraft engines. They are all pushed forwards by the thrust (pushing force) from a jet of something rushing backwards. In rocket and aircraft engines, the jet is hot rushing gases. In water-jet engines, it is spurting water pumped out by an impeller.

☐ JET NOZZLE

The water jet produced by the impeller spurts out of a narrow nozzle at the back of the machine. It is usually hidden below the surface. You can see it here because the jet ski has just hit a wave and bounced up into the air.

Water jet spurts out of nozzle

☐ IMPELLER

As the impeller spins, it sucks water in through an opening beneath the jet ski, speeds it up, and pumps it out backwards.

Water in

Propeller shaft

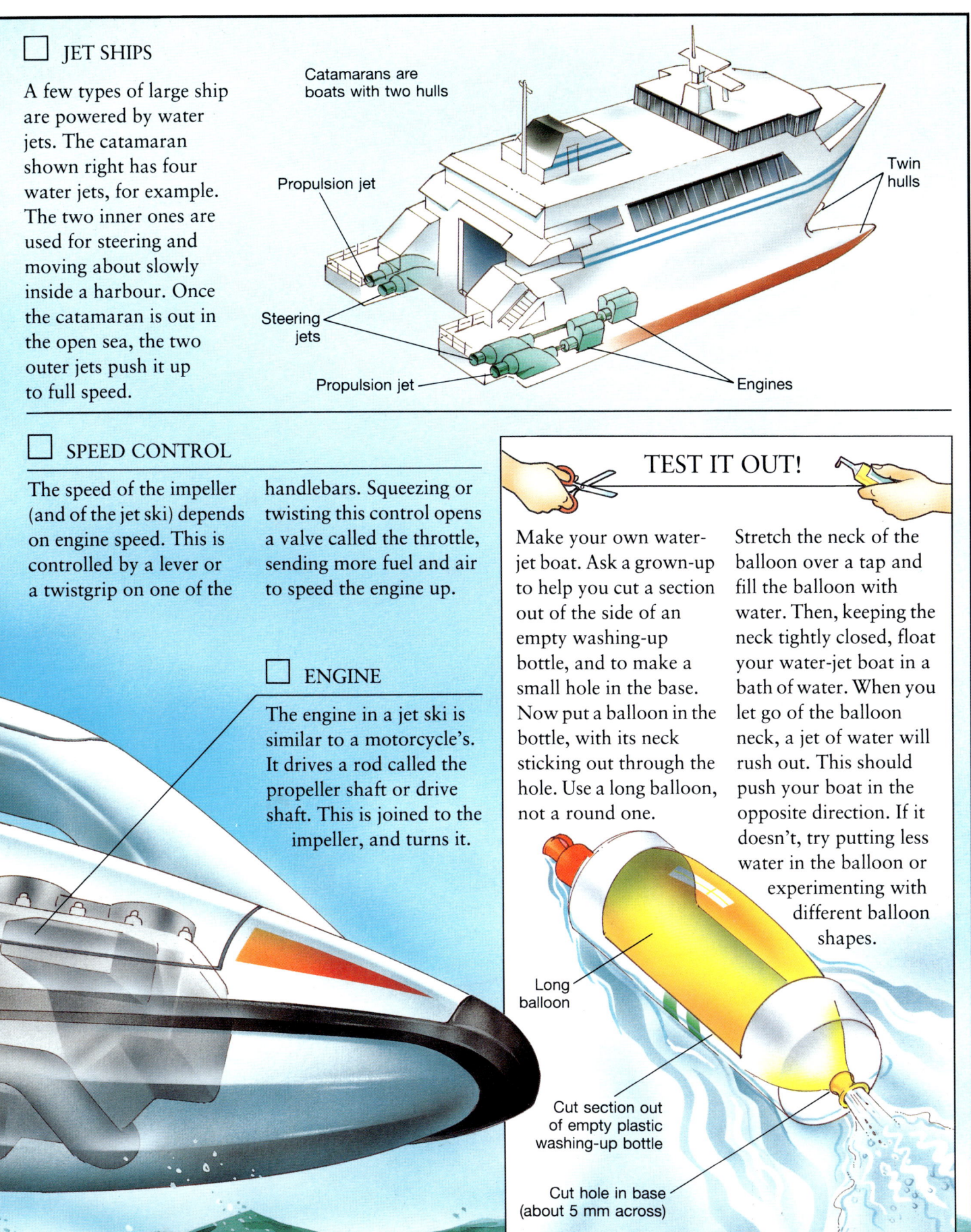

☐ JET SHIPS

A few types of large ship are powered by water jets. The catamaran shown right has four water jets, for example. The two inner ones are used for steering and moving about slowly inside a harbour. Once the catamaran is out in the open sea, the two outer jets push it up to full speed.

Catamarans are boats with two hulls

Propulsion jet

Steering jets

Propulsion jet

Twin hulls

Engines

☐ SPEED CONTROL

The speed of the impeller (and of the jet ski) depends on engine speed. This is controlled by a lever or a twistgrip on one of the handlebars. Squeezing or twisting this control opens a valve called the throttle, sending more fuel and air to speed the engine up.

☐ ENGINE

The engine in a jet ski is similar to a motorcycle's. It drives a rod called the propeller shaft or drive shaft. This is joined to the impeller, and turns it.

TEST IT OUT!

Make your own water-jet boat. Ask a grown-up to help you cut a section out of the side of an empty washing-up bottle, and to make a small hole in the base. Now put a balloon in the bottle, with its neck sticking out through the hole. Use a long balloon, not a round one.

Stretch the neck of the balloon over a tap and fill the balloon with water. Then, keeping the neck tightly closed, float your water-jet boat in a bath of water. When you let go of the balloon neck, a jet of water will rush out. This should push your boat in the opposite direction. If it doesn't, try putting less water in the balloon or experimenting with different balloon shapes.

Long balloon

Cut section out of empty plastic washing-up bottle

Cut hole in base (about 5 mm across)

If boats are left in water, plants and small animals grow on their hulls. This spoils their streamlining and can slow them down. To stop plant and animal growth from fouling (spoiling) them, hulls are regularly painted with an anti-foulant.

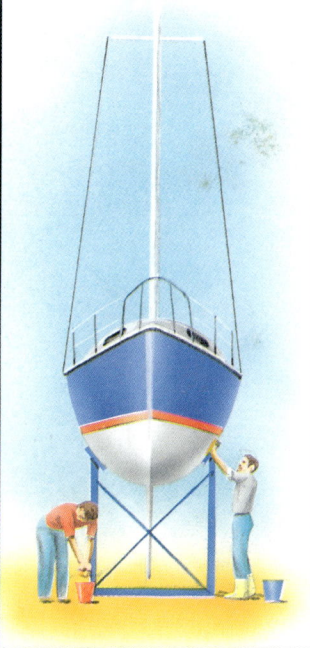

BUILT FOR SPEED

As water flows around a boat, it rubs against the hull. This creates a force called drag which tries to slow the boat down. If the hull is streamlined, so that its surfaces are smooth and curved, the water rubs less and drag is reduced.

As a boat goes faster, the effect of drag becomes stronger. This means that streamlining is particularly important for powerboats, racing yachts, and any other boat designed to travel at superfast speeds.

Long thin
hull helps
streamlining

☐ TWIN HULLS

The powerboat shown here has two narrow hulls instead of a single large one. This puts a smaller area of hull in contact with the water, cutting down on drag and helping the boat to cut through the water more easily.

☐ STREAMLINING

The boat's hulls are carefully shaped, with smooth gentle curves. There are no sharp edges to break up the flow of the water over them. Before each race, the hulls are polished to make them even smoother.

ALL SORTS OF HULLS

Most boats have a single hull, but boats with more than one hull are becoming quite popular.

Multihulls slip through the water more easily and they are steadier in bad weather conditions.

HULL RECORDS

A four-hull powerboat called a quadrimaran is being built in France, to try to make the fastest Atlantic crossing.

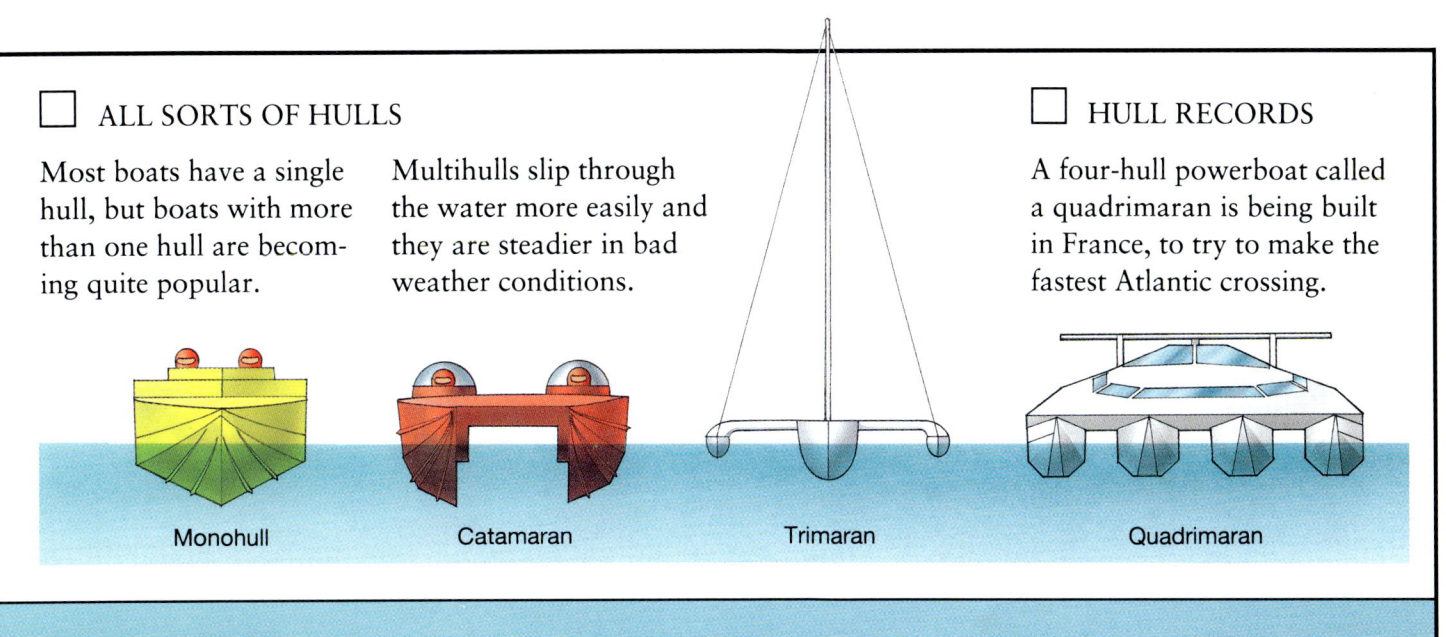

Monohull · Catamaran · Trimaran · Quadrimaran

Streamlined cockpit built into each hull

ENGINES

On this boat, each propeller has its own big and powerful diesel engine. The engines are called inboard, because they are inside the hulls.

Less powerful boats have smaller, petrol engines. If the engines are fitted outside the hull, at the boat's stern, they are called outboard motors.

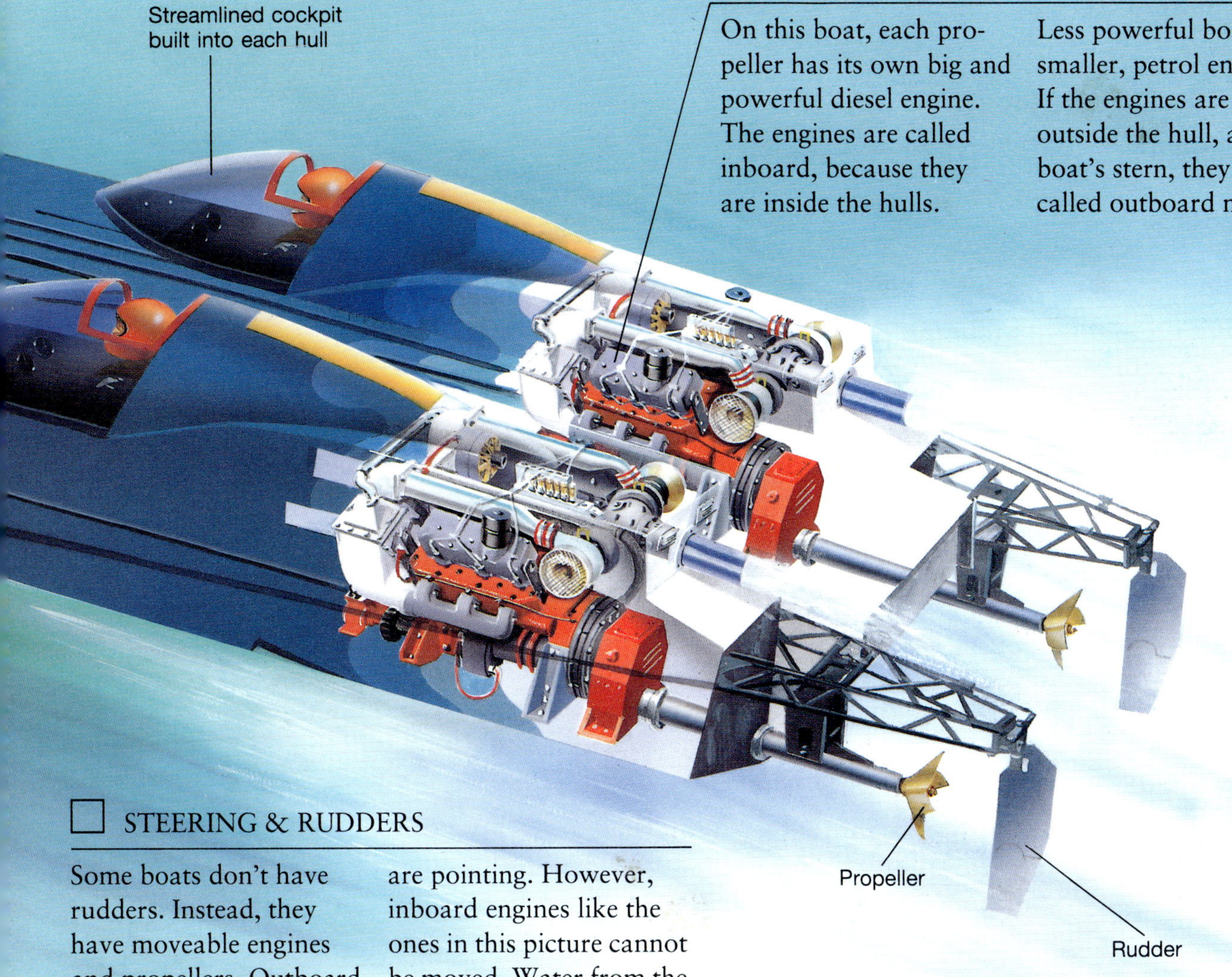

Propeller

Rudder

STEERING & RUDDERS

Some boats don't have rudders. Instead, they have moveable engines and propellers. Outboard motors work like this. The boat goes wherever the engine and propeller are pointing. However, inboard engines like the ones in this picture cannot be moved. Water from the propellers pushes against the rudders, turning the boat (see pages 14-15).

FOCUS ON KNOTS

Speed at sea is measured in knots (1 knot equals 1.85 km/h). The term comes from an old way of measuring. A piece of wood was tied to a rope knotted every 14.4 metres – one knot at 14.4, two at 28.8, three at 43.2, and so on. When the wood was thrown into the sea it pulled the rope after it. Counting the knots dragged out in 28 seconds gave the ship's speed.

HYDROFOILS

One way of getting rid of the drag between water and a boat is to raise the hull out of the water altogether. Boats called hydrofoils do this by using aerofoil-shaped underwater wings called foils. At low speeds, a hydrofoil floats normally. But as it speeds up, the foils begin to create a suction force called lift. This acts upwards, pushing the hull higher. If the hydrofoil travels quickly enough, its hull rises out of the water completely.

☐ JET POWER

The hydrofoil illustrated here has water-jet engines which work in much the same way as those in jet skis (see pages 18-19). Other types of hydrofoil are powered by engine-driven propellers. Hydrofoils powered by water jets are also called jetfoils.

Water-jet engine

Steering flap

Rear strut

Rear foil

Water intake

☐ STRUTS FOR STRENGTH

Uprights called struts are joined to the hull and connected to the water intake by the rear foils. This results in a strong structure which can bear the whole weight of the hydrofoil. The moveable flaps on the struts and foils are used for steering.

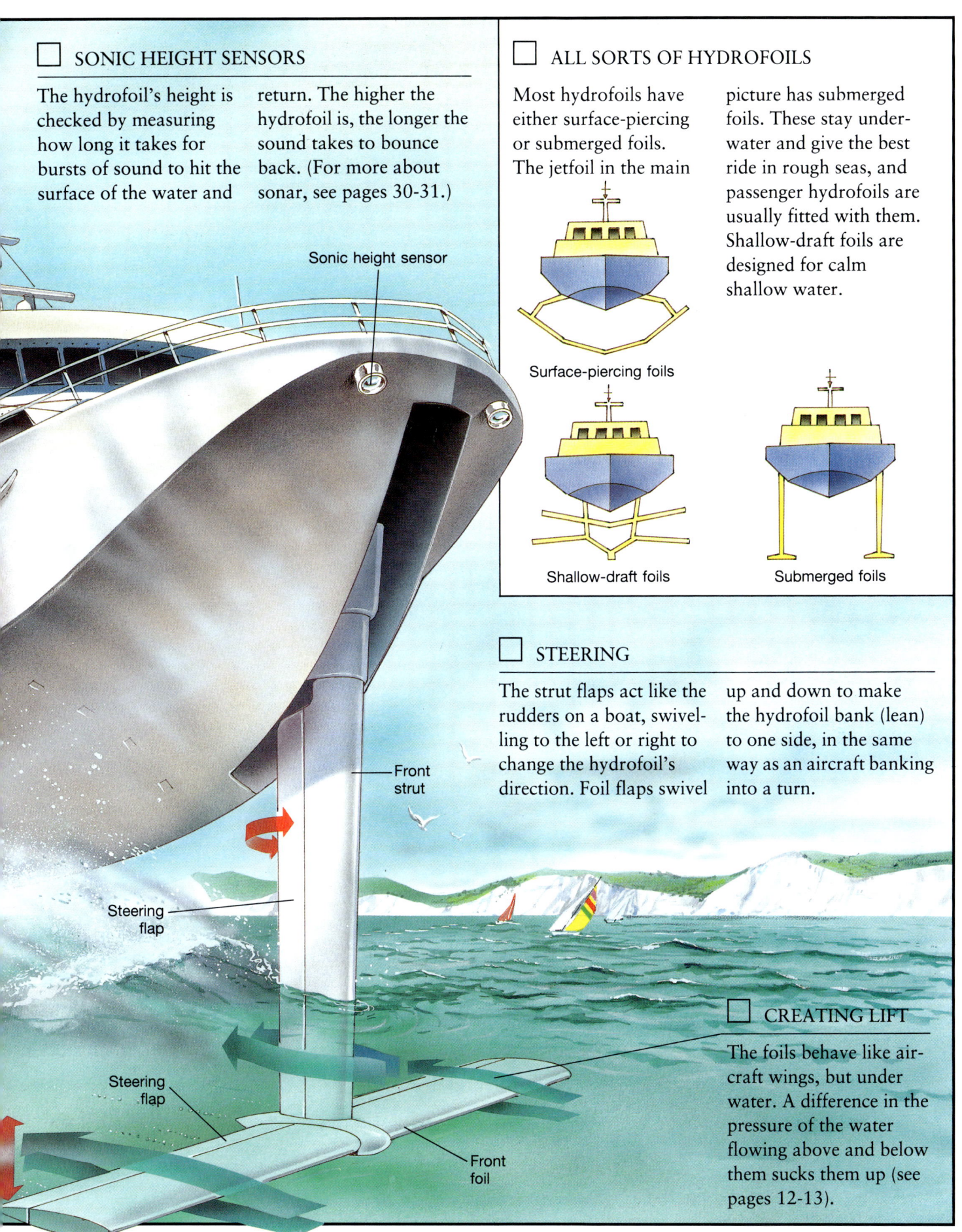

SONIC HEIGHT SENSORS

The hydrofoil's height is checked by measuring how long it takes for bursts of sound to hit the surface of the water and return. The higher the hydrofoil is, the longer the sound takes to bounce back. (For more about sonar, see pages 30-31.)

Sonic height sensor

ALL SORTS OF HYDROFOILS

Most hydrofoils have either surface-piercing or submerged foils. The jetfoil in the main picture has submerged foils. These stay underwater and give the best ride in rough seas, and passenger hydrofoils are usually fitted with them. Shallow-draft foils are designed for calm shallow water.

Surface-piercing foils

Shallow-draft foils

Submerged foils

STEERING

The strut flaps act like the rudders on a boat, swivelling to the left or right to change the hydrofoil's direction. Foil flaps swivel up and down to make the hydrofoil bank (lean) to one side, in the same way as an aircraft banking into a turn.

Front strut

Steering flap

Steering flap

Front foil

CREATING LIFT

The foils behave like aircraft wings, but under water. A difference in the pressure of the water flowing above and below them sucks them up (see pages 12-13).

FOCUS ON CUSHIONS

A hovercraft gives a smoother ride than a ship because it travels above the waves that make ships roll about. A hovercraft can do this because a cushion of air under its hull holds it above the water.

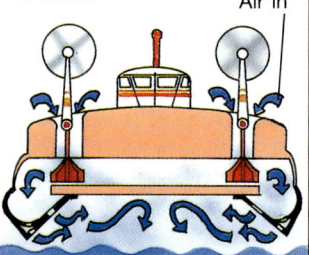

Hovercraft rides on cushion of air

A flexible (stretchy) skirt traps more air inside, and makes the cushion deeper.

HOVERCRAFT

Although a hydrofoil can lift its hull out of the water, other parts stay submerged, so there is still some water drag slowing it down. The only solution to this drag problem is to get out of the water altogether, and fly – and that's what a hovercraft does.

Without the slowing effect of water drag, a hovercraft can travel faster than ships. The world's fastest ferries can manage 30 knots (55.5 km/h). The SR.N4 passenger hovercraft crosses the English Channel at an average speed of 65 knots!

Flight deck

TEST IT OUT!

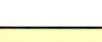

To see how a hovercraft works, get an ice-cream container and ask a grown-up to help you cut a hole in the base, just big enough to take the nozzle of a hair dryer. Now place the upturned container on a dry flat surface. Hold the nozzle in the hole and switch on the hair dryer. The container will start to hover!

Don't do this near water!

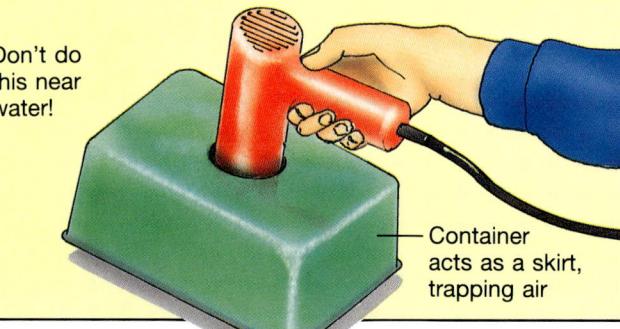

Container acts as a skirt, trapping air

☐ FLIGHT DECK

The flight deck of a large hovercraft is like a cross between the cockpit of an aircraft and a ship's bridge. All the instruments needed to control the hovercraft are here.

Passenger cabin

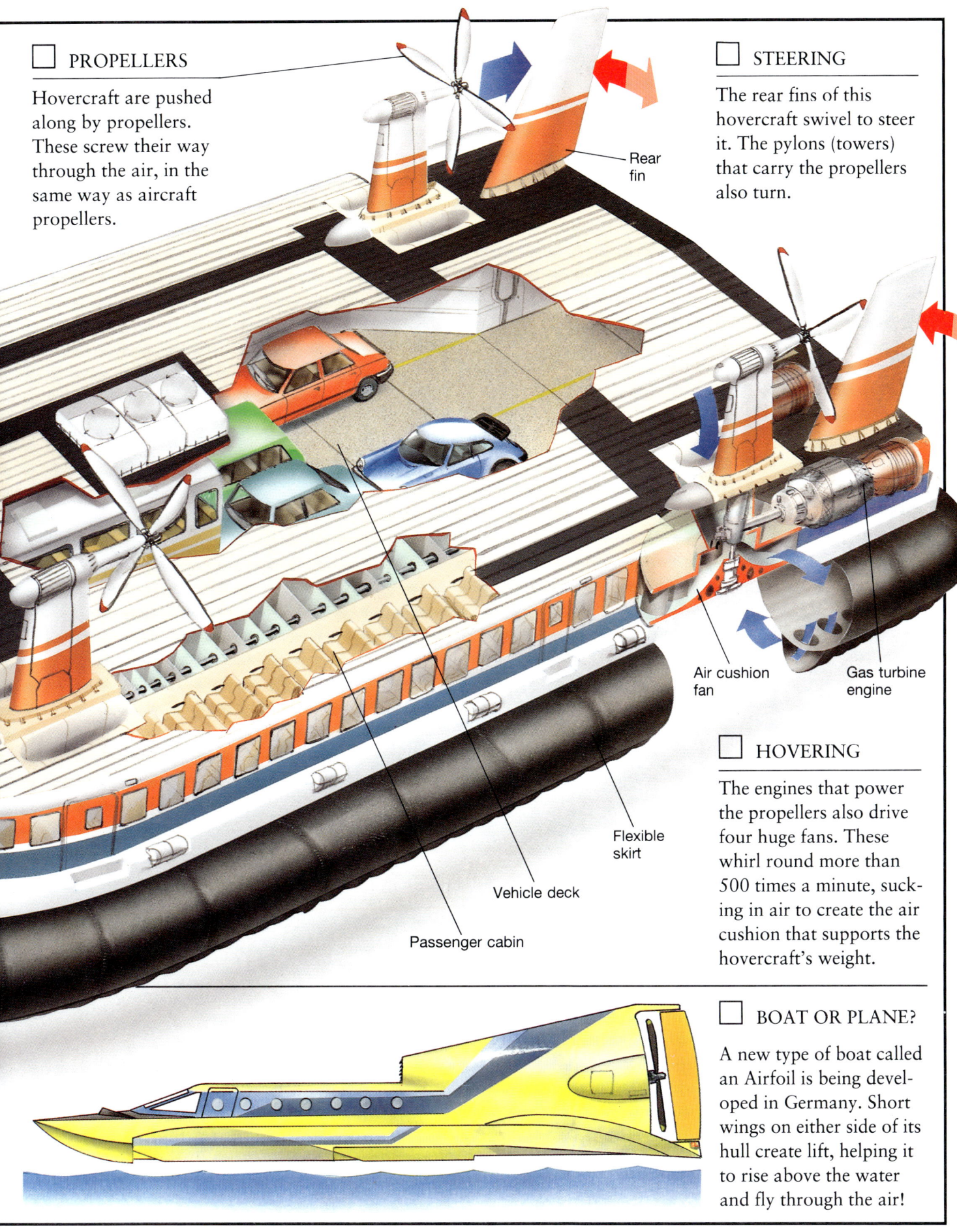

PROPELLERS

Hovercraft are pushed along by propellers. These screw their way through the air, in the same way as aircraft propellers.

STEERING

The rear fins of this hovercraft swivel to steer it. The pylons (towers) that carry the propellers also turn.

Rear fin

Air cushion fan

Gas turbine engine

HOVERING

The engines that power the propellers also drive four huge fans. These whirl round more than 500 times a minute, sucking in air to create the air cushion that supports the hovercraft's weight.

Flexible skirt

Vehicle deck

Passenger cabin

BOAT OR PLANE?

A new type of boat called an Airfoil is being developed in Germany. Short wings on either side of its hull create lift, helping it to rise above the water and fly through the air!

☐ GAS TURBINES

As air enters a gas turbine engine, it is compressed (squeezed). Fuel is mixed with the air in a combustion chamber. Then the mixture is burnt, to create hot gases which shoot out of the engine, spinning the turbine blades.

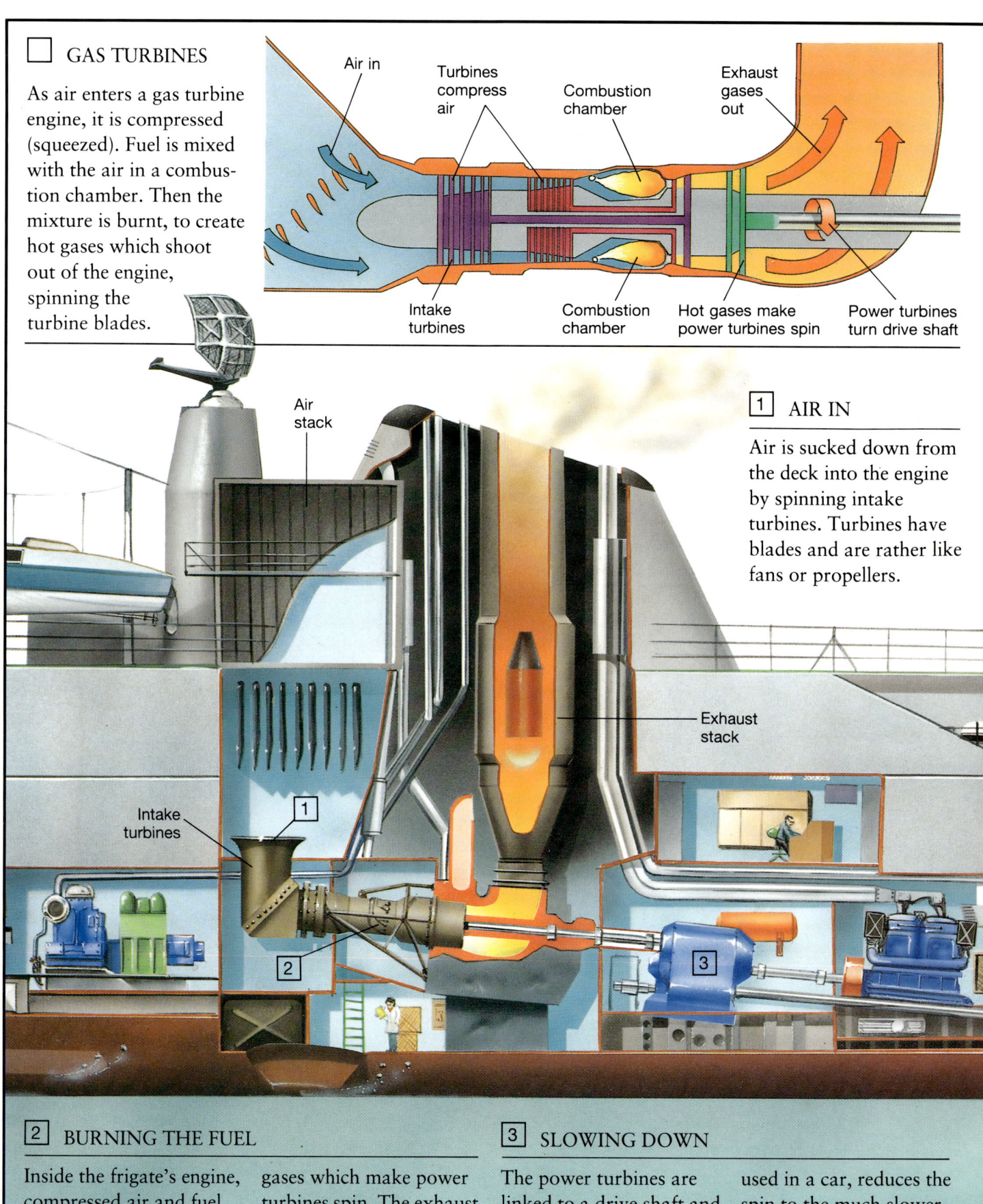

Air in

Turbines compress air

Combustion chamber

Exhaust gases out

Intake turbines

Combustion chamber

Hot gases make power turbines spin

Power turbines turn drive shaft

Air stack

Exhaust stack

Intake turbines

1 AIR IN

Air is sucked down from the deck into the engine by spinning intake turbines. Turbines have blades and are rather like fans or propellers.

2 BURNING THE FUEL

Inside the frigate's engine, compressed air and fuel are mixed and lit. The mixture explodes, creating gases which make power turbines spin. The exhaust gases then escape up a stack (chimney).

3 SLOWING DOWN

The power turbines are linked to a drive shaft and make it spin at high speed. A gearbox, like the type used in a car, reduces the spin to the much slower speed needed by the ship's propeller.

THE ENGINE ROOM

All boats, apart from sailing ships, need engines to propel them through the water. A few large boats have water-jet engines, and a few have nuclear engines. But most are powered by diesel or gas turbine engines, or both.

The diesel engines fitted in ships are like the ones used in trains and trucks, only bigger and more powerful. Gas turbines produce more power for their weight than any other kind of ship's engine, though, so they allow room for extra passengers and cargo. Gas turbines work in a similar way to a jet aircraft's engines.

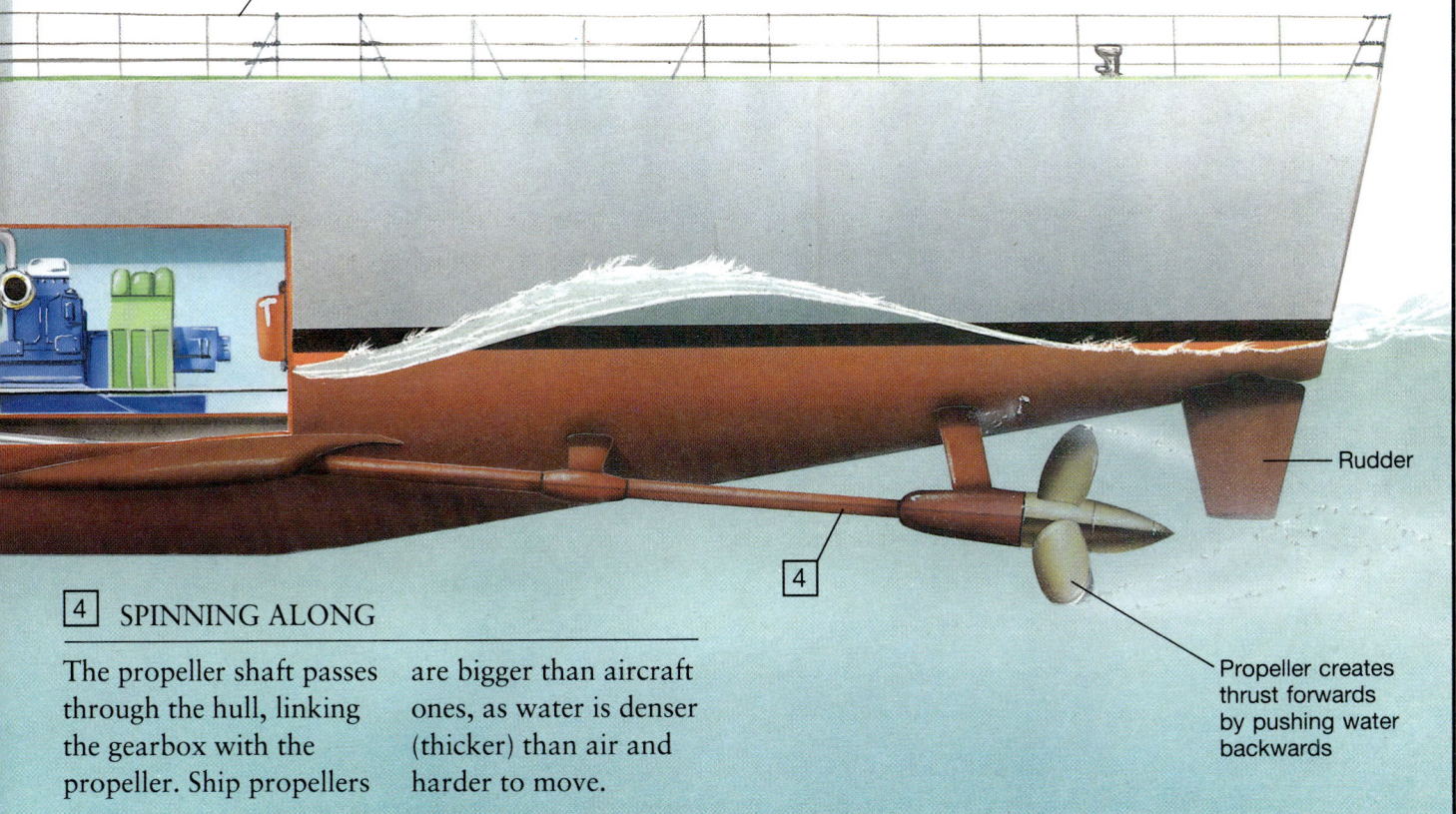

FOCUS ON NUCLEAR POWER

Nuclear submarine

A few of the biggest military ships and submarines are propelled by nuclear power. The advantage of nuclear engines is that they can go for months without needing to be refuelled.

These engines work by making nuclear fuel give off heat, which is used to turn water into steam. The steam drives turbines linked to the propeller.

☐ POWERING WARSHIPS

Many warships are fitted with gas turbine engines. The frigate illustrated here is a typical medium-sized military vessel. Even though it may weigh as much as 5000 tonnes, one gas turbine engine (or two at most) is enough to propel it.

Rudder

4 SPINNING ALONG

The propeller shaft passes through the hull, linking the gearbox with the propeller. Ship propellers are bigger than aircraft ones, as water is denser (thicker) than air and harder to move.

Propeller creates thrust forwards by pushing water backwards

FOCUS ON
SINS

All submarines and many big ships have a Ship's Inertial Navigation System (SINS) which keeps them on course. (Navigation means finding a way.)

Subs need 3 gyroscopes

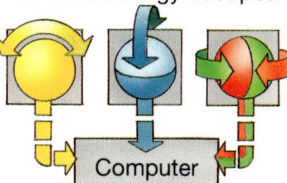

Computer

SINS uses one or more gyroscopes (wheels that spin) in special frames. They always point in the same direction, even if the ship or sub (and therefore the frame) turns. SINS works out the vessel's position from its speed, and from differences between the way it and the gyroscopes are pointing.

ON THE BRIDGE

The bridge is where the officers steer and control the ship. It is high up so they get a clear view of other vessels nearby. All the information collected by the various instruments on board is brought together on the bridge, so that the officers can sail as safely as possible. A lot of ships now have electronic aids which show information on computer screens. Many of the systems automatically warn of faults in machinery, or of dangers such as shallow water.

1 Captain	6 Autopilot steers the ship automatically (course is set on dial)	11 Bow thruster (see page 16)
2 First Officer		12 ISIS (Integrated Ship Instrumentation System) checks engine
3 Computerized chart	7 Indicators show rudder position	
4 Telephones let officers talk to crew throughout the ship and, by radio, to people on land	8 Tiller control to move the rudders	13 LSR (Live Situation Report) shows information, and reminds officers to check instruments
	9 Magnetic compass (used if SINS gyroscope fails)	
5 Chart table for plotting the ship's course (linked to no. 3)	10 Engine speed controls	14 Radar screen

☐ SATELLITE NAVIGATION

Many ships now use a navigation system called GPS (short for Global, or world, Positioning System). GPS is sent information by radio from satellites circling the Earth. It uses the information to work out ships' positions and to keep them on course.

Signals are sent by three satellites

Satellite

Satellite

Satellite

Ships would collide without warning messages from satellites

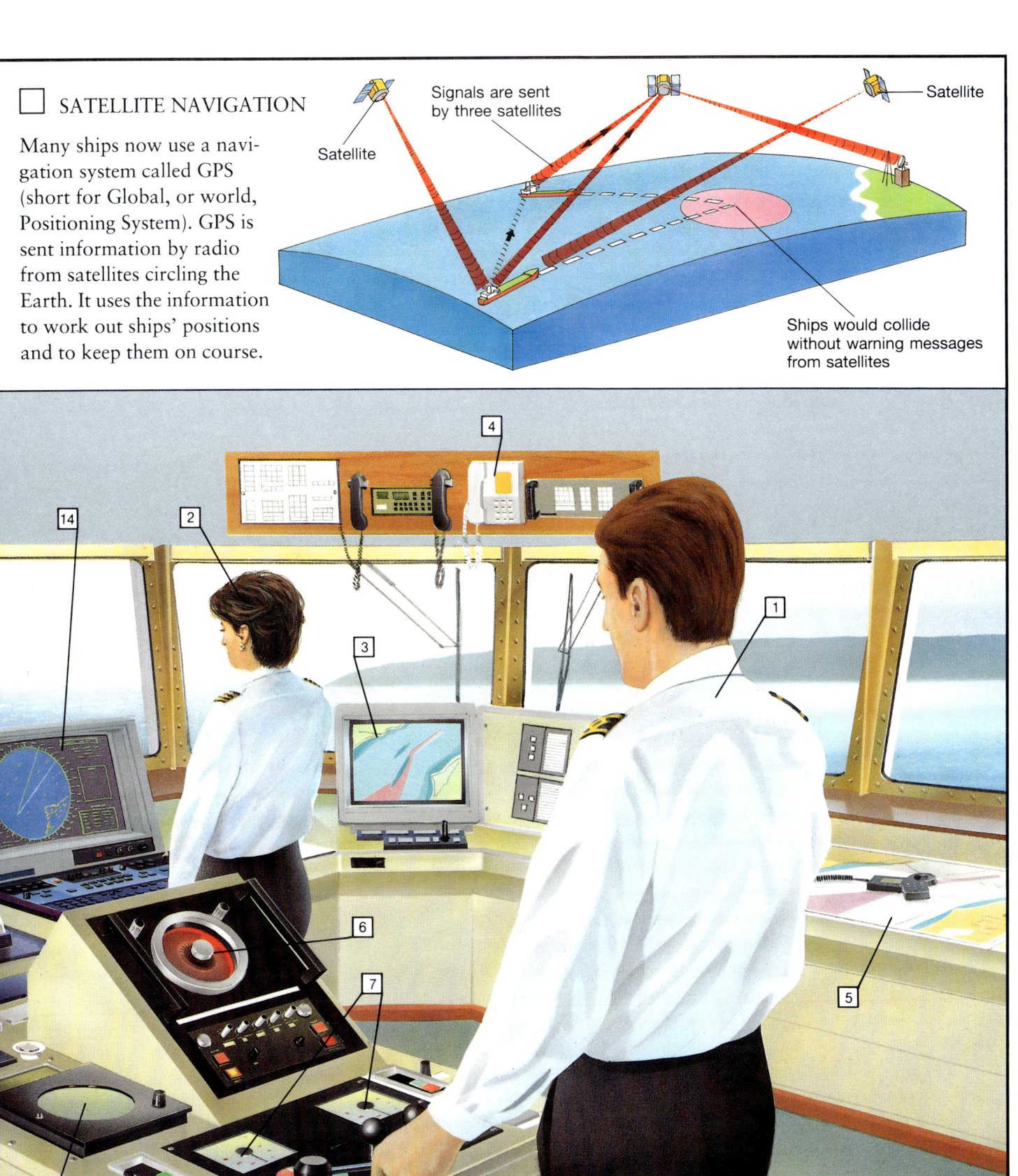

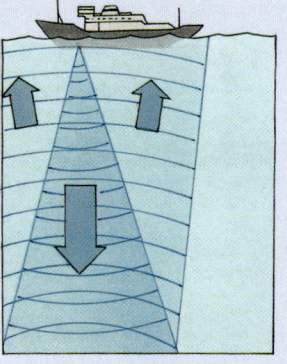

Sonar works because sound waves bounce off solid objects and send back echoes (sonar is also called echolocation). If sound waves are beamed down into the sea, they bounce off the seabed back up to the ship.

Echoes bounce back

Sonar waves hit seabed

Sonar equipment uses the time gap between sending out the sound waves and receiving their echoes to work out how far away the seabed is. Shoals of fish are also picked up by sonar.

Sonar screen on bridge

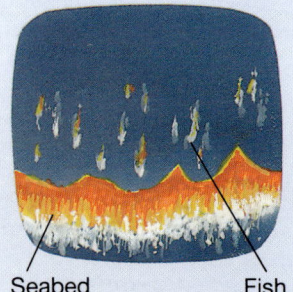

Seabed   Fish

SEEING WITH SOUND

We see the world around us because light bounces off things into our eyes. However, light does not travel through water as easily as it does through air, and this makes it more difficult to see underwater. Sonar is a system that uses sound instead of light to 'see'. The word sonar is made from SOund Navigation And Ranging. Ranging means measuring distance.

☐ ACTIVE SONAR

Active sonar works by sending out bursts of sound and picking up any echoes that bounce back from objects in the sound waves' path. The sonar sounds are so high that they are far beyond the highest notes we can hear with our ears.

Sonar helps trawler to find shoals of fish

Submarine's passive sonar picks up noise from ship's engine

☐ PASSIVE SONAR

This system doesn't send out sound waves, it just listens to them. Passive sonar is used by vessels like submarines which want to keep their position a secret. If active sonar was used, the sound waves would be picked up by the sonar systems of nearby ships.

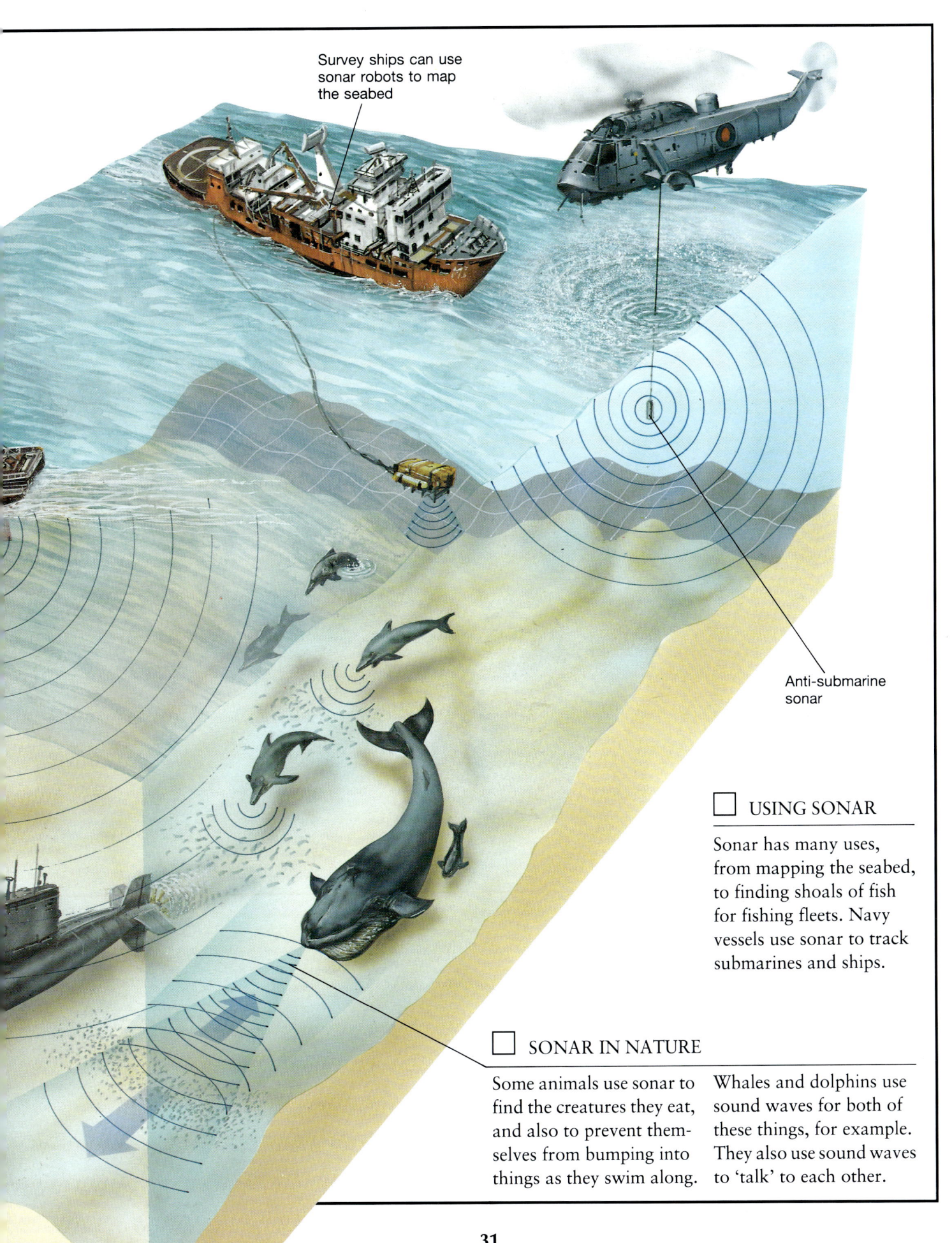

Survey ships can use sonar robots to map the seabed

Anti-submarine sonar

☐ USING SONAR

Sonar has many uses, from mapping the seabed, to finding shoals of fish for fishing fleets. Navy vessels use sonar to track submarines and ships.

☐ SONAR IN NATURE

Some animals use sonar to find the creatures they eat, and also to prevent themselves from bumping into things as they swim along. Whales and dolphins use sound waves for both of these things, for example. They also use sound waves to 'talk' to each other.

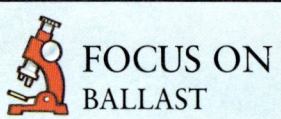

FOCUS ON BALLAST

Ballast is the extra weight that makes a submarine sink. It is usually sea water, taken in and stored in tanks. In 1960, the *Trieste* made the world's deepest dive (to almost 11,000 metres, in the Pacific Ocean) using petrol, sea water and iron shot as ballast.

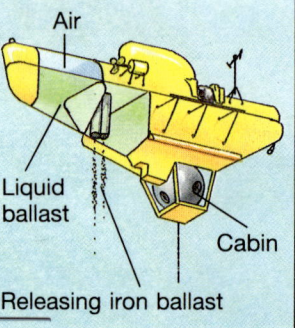

Air

Liquid ballast

Cabin

Releasing iron ballast

SUBMARINES

Unlike other types of floating machine, submarines are specially designed so that they can sink! Submarines have to be able to float too, of course, so that they can rise back up to the surface again. They control their depth with ballast, using it to make themselves heavier or lighter than the sea water around them.

Submarines have to be strong enough to resist the crushing pressure of water, particularly because this gets worse the deeper they go.

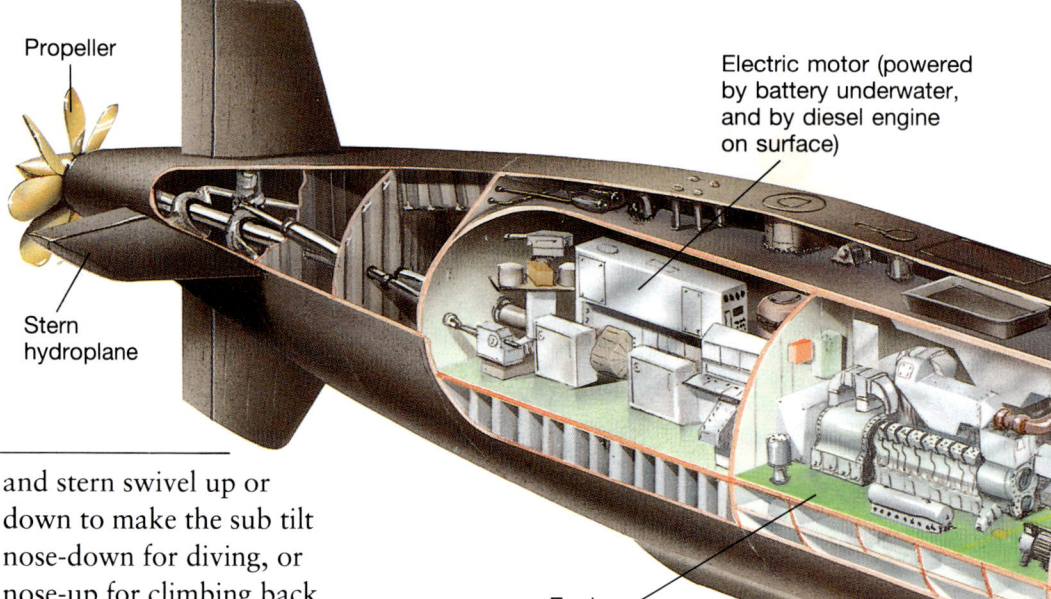

Propeller

Stern hydroplane

Electric motor (powered by battery underwater, and by diesel engine on surface)

Engine room

☐ STEERING

Like ships, submarines have rudders to steer them to port (left) or starboard (right). Short wings called hydroplanes at the bow and stern swivel up or down to make the sub tilt nose-down for diving, or nose-up for climbing back towards the surface.

☐ DIVING & SURFACING

When a vent at the top of the ballast tanks is opened, air rushes out. Water then surges in to take its place, through vents at the bottom of the tanks. The extra weight makes the submarine sink. When the water is forced out by pumping in air, the sub rises again.

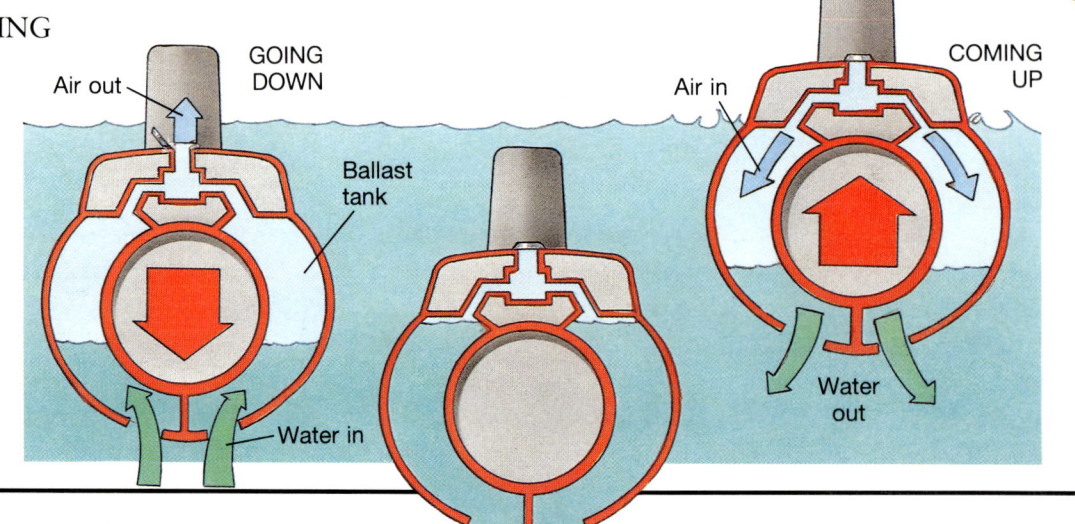

Air out

GOING DOWN

Ballast tank

Water in

Air in

COMING UP

Water out

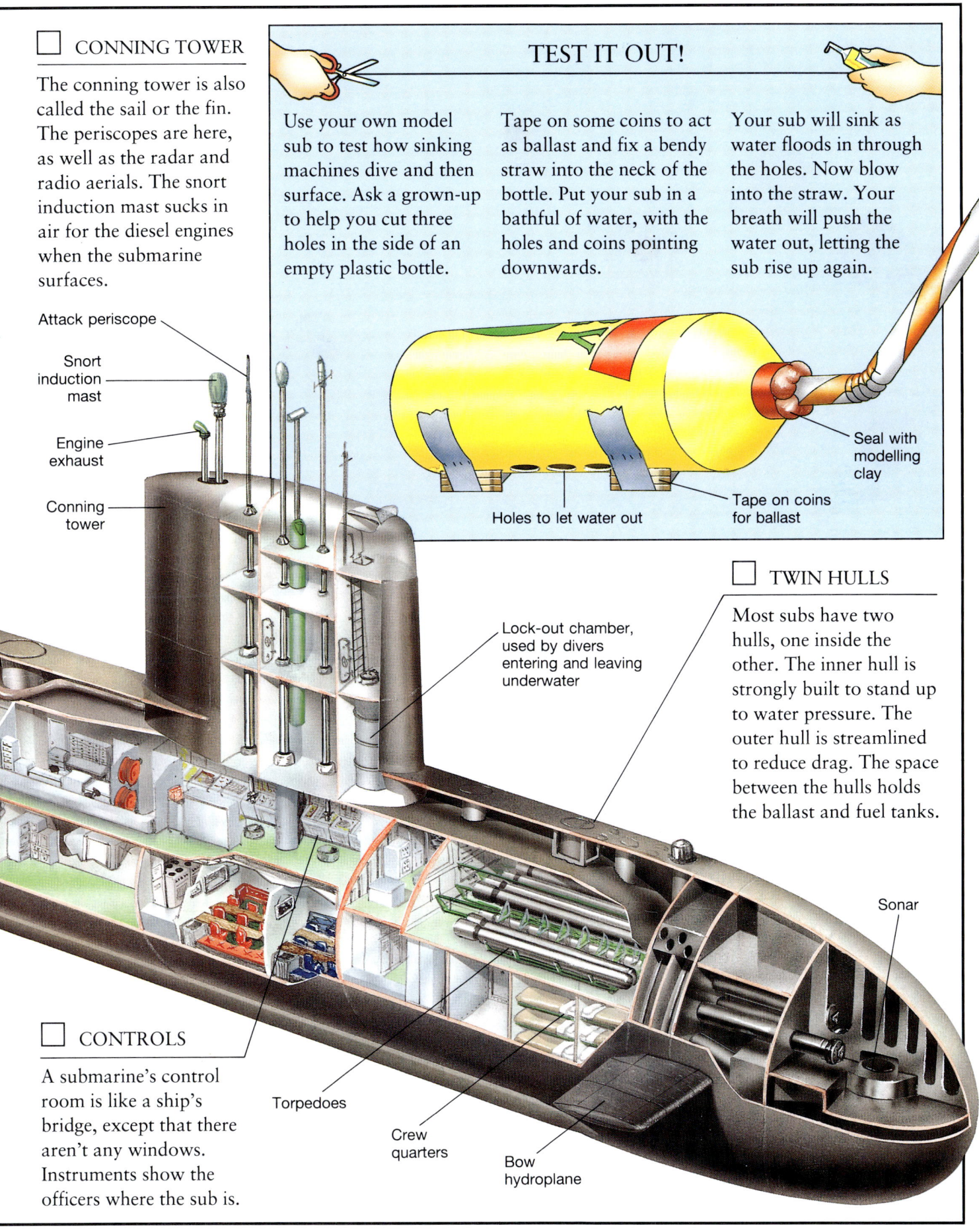

CONNING TOWER

The conning tower is also called the sail or the fin. The periscopes are here, as well as the radar and radio aerials. The snort induction mast sucks in air for the diesel engines when the submarine surfaces.

Attack periscope

Snort induction mast

Engine exhaust

Conning tower

TEST IT OUT!

Use your own model sub to test how sinking machines dive and then surface. Ask a grown-up to help you cut three holes in the side of an empty plastic bottle.

Tape on some coins to act as ballast and fix a bendy straw into the neck of the bottle. Put your sub in a bathful of water, with the holes and coins pointing downwards.

Your sub will sink as water floods in through the holes. Now blow into the straw. Your breath will push the water out, letting the sub rise up again.

Seal with modelling clay

Holes to let water out

Tape on coins for ballast

Lock-out chamber, used by divers entering and leaving underwater

TWIN HULLS

Most subs have two hulls, one inside the other. The inner hull is strongly built to stand up to water pressure. The outer hull is streamlined to reduce drag. The space between the hulls holds the ballast and fuel tanks.

Sonar

CONTROLS

A submarine's control room is like a ship's bridge, except that there aren't any windows. Instruments show the officers where the sub is.

Torpedoes

Crew quarters

Bow hydroplane

Water pressure increases with depth because the deeper you go in the ocean, the more water there is pressing down on you from above. At 3785 metres, where the wreck of the liner *Titanic* lies, the water pressure is 350 times that at the surface.

EXPLORING THE DEEP

Submersibles are much smaller than submarines, but they can dive to far greater depths. The submersible *Alvin* has reached 4000 metres, for example. Diesel-electric submarines can only go to 150-200 metres.

Unlike submarines, which are used for military work by the world's navies, submersibles do all sorts of underwater jobs. As well as laying, inspecting and repairing underwater pipelines and telephone cables, submersibles are used to service oil rigs, to map the ocean floor, and to find and survey shipwrecks. In 1985, for example, *Alvin* discovered the wreck of the liner *Titanic*, which had collided with an iceberg and sunk in the Atlantic Ocean in April 1912.

Submersibles are also used by scientists to study the curious plants and animals of the ocean depths.

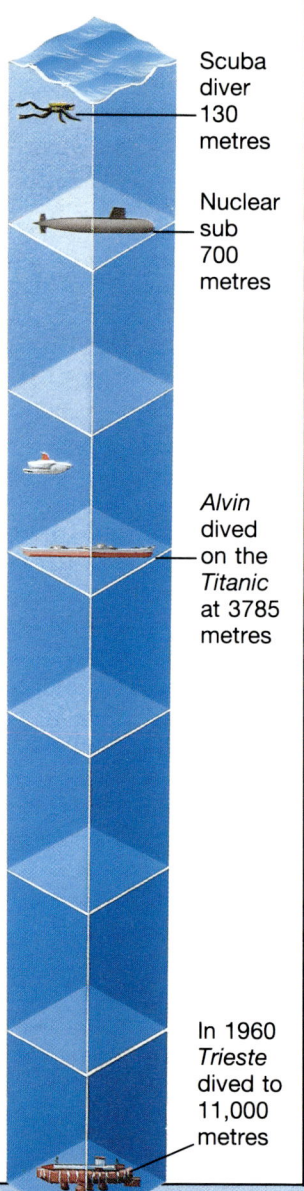

Scuba diver 130 metres

Nuclear sub 700 metres

Alvin dived on the *Titanic* at 3785 metres

In 1960 *Trieste* dived to 11,000 metres

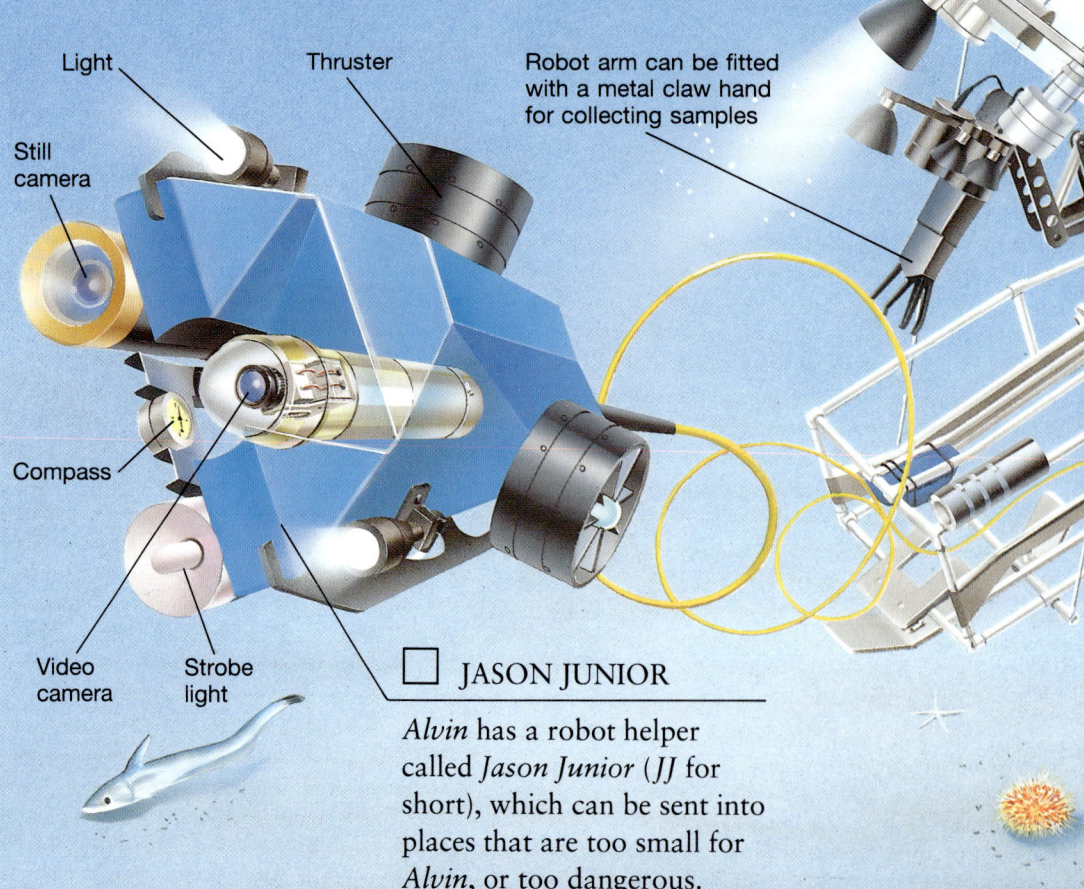

Light

Thruster

Robot arm can be fitted with a metal claw hand for collecting samples

Still camera

Compass

Video camera

Strobe light

JASON JUNIOR

Alvin has a robot helper called *Jason Junior* (*JJ* for short), which can be sent into places that are too small for *Alvin*, or too dangerous.

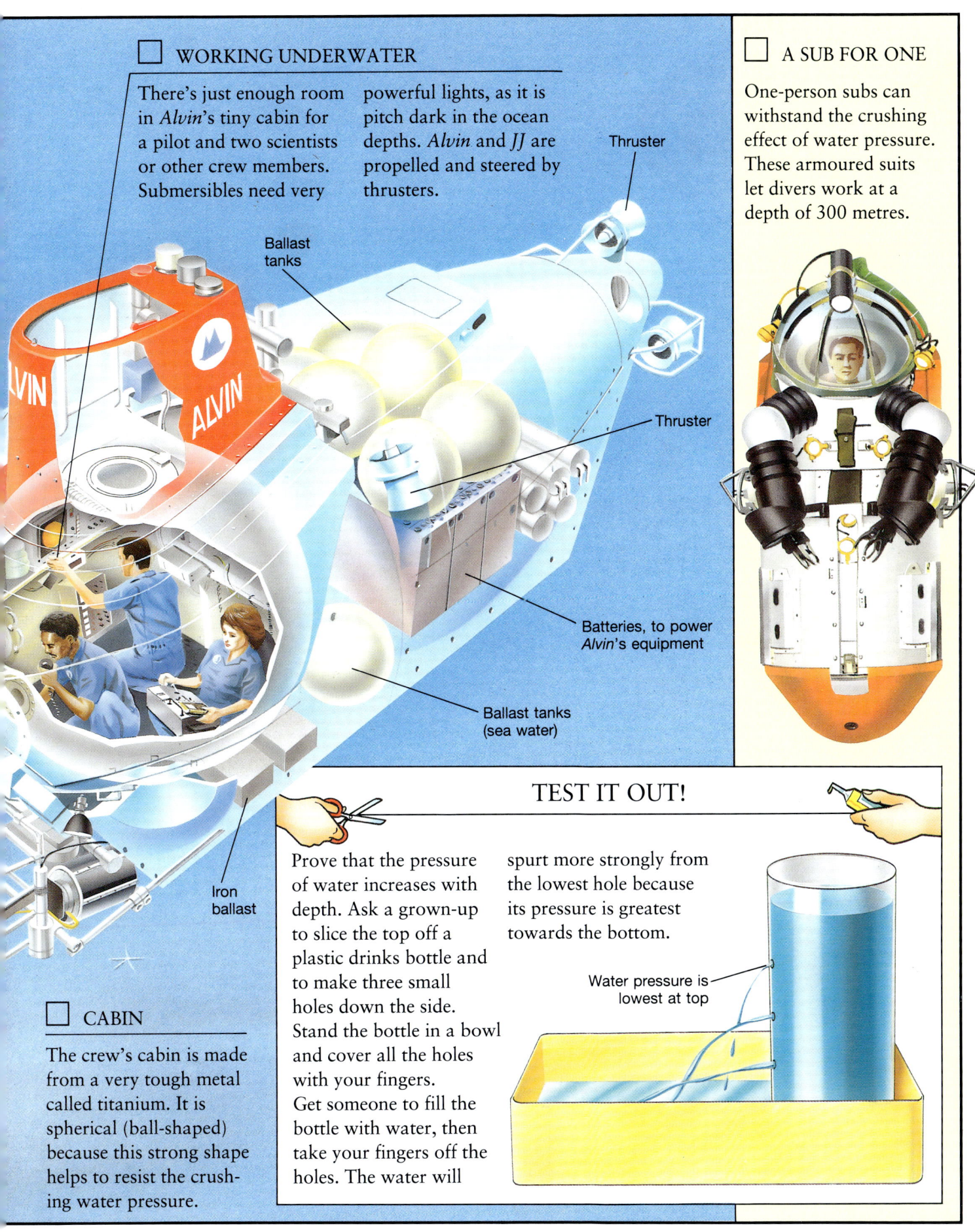

☐ WORKING UNDERWATER

There's just enough room in *Alvin*'s tiny cabin for a pilot and two scientists or other crew members. Submersibles need very powerful lights, as it is pitch dark in the ocean depths. *Alvin* and *JJ* are propelled and steered by thrusters.

Thruster

Ballast tanks

ALVIN

Thruster

Batteries, to power *Alvin*'s equipment

Ballast tanks (sea water)

Iron ballast

☐ CABIN

The crew's cabin is made from a very tough metal called titanium. It is spherical (ball-shaped) because this strong shape helps to resist the crushing water pressure.

☐ A SUB FOR ONE

One-person subs can withstand the crushing effect of water pressure. These armoured suits let divers work at a depth of 300 metres.

TEST IT OUT!

Prove that the pressure of water increases with depth. Ask a grown-up to slice the top off a plastic drinks bottle and to make three small holes down the side. Stand the bottle in a bowl and cover all the holes with your fingers. Get someone to fill the bottle with water, then take your fingers off the holes. The water will spurt more strongly from the lowest hole because its pressure is greatest towards the bottom.

Water pressure is lowest at top

☐ BUILT FOR STRENGTH

Lifeboat hulls must be strong enough to stand up to the battering they suffer in rough seas. The first lifeboats had wooden hulls, but today many of them have steel ones. The *Arun* was the first British lifeboat to have a glass-reinforced plastic hull.

Radio aerial

Radar aerial

Helm

52

☐ STAYING AFLOAT

A lifeboat is designed to keep floating even if it hits something and is holed. Its hull is divided into watertight boxes called compartments. When one of these is holed, it fills with water. The others stay watertight and keep the boat afloat.

☐ KEEPING THE RIGHT WAY UP

Arun class lifeboats are self-righting – they turn upright again if they capsize in rough seas.

Water ballast at the hull bottom helps to keep the boat upright (1). If it rolls (2), this ballast pours into a righting tank (3). The extra weight on one side of the boat rolls it back upright again (4).

1

Righting tank

Ballast tank

2

3

4

SAFETY AT SEA

Ships are very safe, but sometimes a vessel may face an emergency which the crew cannot handle without help. There might be a serious fire on board. If its engines fail, a boat might be blown towards rocks. A yacht might be caught in a sudden storm. At these desperate times, lifeboats may be sent out to rescue them.

There are different classes of lifeboat. The boat illustrated here is an *Arun* class boat. It was specially designed for the Royal National Lifeboat Institute (RNLI). This organization saves lives at sea all round the British and Irish coasts. Its lifeboats must be able to carry on working when the weather is so bad that other vessels can't put to sea.

Life-raft

FOCUS ON SWATH

Stable ships are ones that do not roll about much. They are safer and more comfortable to sail in. A new ship called a SWATH (Small Waterplane Area Twin Hull) is very big and stable. Together, its width and twin-hull design cut down the rolling.

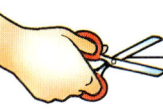

TEST IT OUT!

Buoys are floating markers used to warn ships of dangers such as shallow water. You can make one from a ping-pong ball. Ask a grown-up to cut a small hole in the ball.

Stick some modelling clay inside and push in a toothpick flag. Float your buoy in water and make some waves. The clay acts like the lifeboat's ballast to keep the buoy upright.

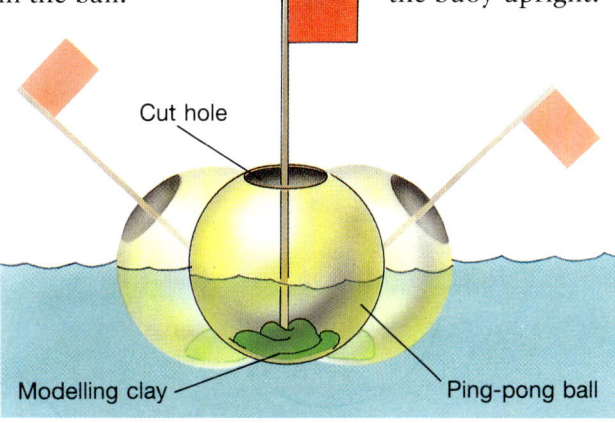

Cut hole

Modelling clay

Ping-pong ball

PORTS & HARBOURS

Ships call in at ports to be repaired and cleaned, and to take on and off-load passengers, cargo and fuel. A port must be close to main roads and a railway so that people and goods can get to and from it easily and quickly.

The world's biggest and busiest ports cover vast areas, and there are always great numbers of ships arriving and leaving. Each year more than 35,000 ships enter and leave the port of Singapore in the Far East. That's almost 100 ships every day, seven days a week, all year round!

☐ MARINA

A marina is a special mooring place for yachts and other pleasure and sports boats.

☐ RO-RO FERRIES

Passengers can drive their cars straight from the quayside on or off roll-on roll-off ferries (ro-ros).

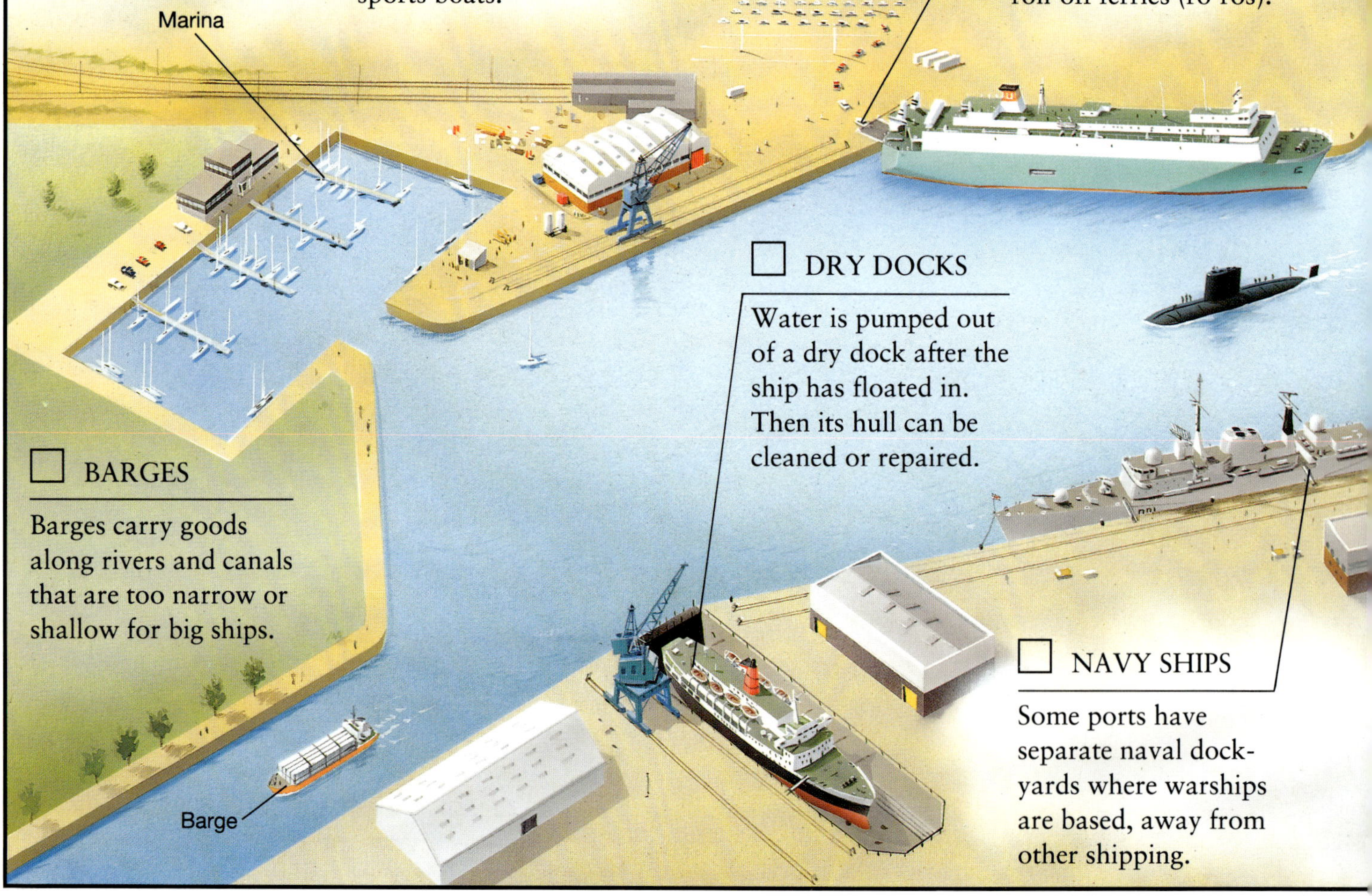

Marina

☐ DRY DOCKS

Water is pumped out of a dry dock after the ship has floated in. Then its hull can be cleaned or repaired.

☐ BARGES

Barges carry goods along rivers and canals that are too narrow or shallow for big ships.

☐ NAVY SHIPS

Some ports have separate naval dock-yards where warships are based, away from other shipping.

Barge

☐ HEAVY LIFTERS

Some ships are designed to transport heavy loads, including other ships. One type sinks until the load can float over its deck. When the ship rises back up again, the load is safely on board.

Tugboat

☐ OIL TERMINAL

Oil is carried around the world by sea. Many ports have oil terminals nearby, where tankers can load or unload into storage tanks.

☐ TRAFFIC CONTROL

The position and movements of each ship are watched carefully, using radar, so that traffic moves freely and there are no accidents. Radar works like sonar, but with radio waves.

☐ HOVERPORT

Hovercraft travel on land and water. They skim across the sea and up slopes on to dry land at special hoverports.

☐ CONTAINERS

Container ships dock alongside quays with special cranes for loading and unloading their cargo containers.

INDEX

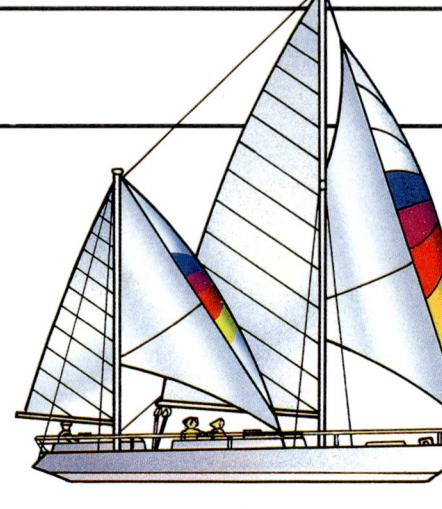

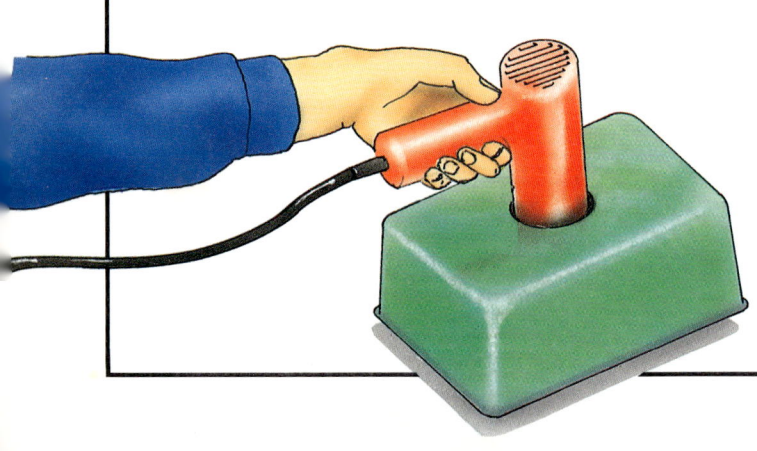